LEGENDS OF MY PEOPLE
THE GREAT OJIBWAY

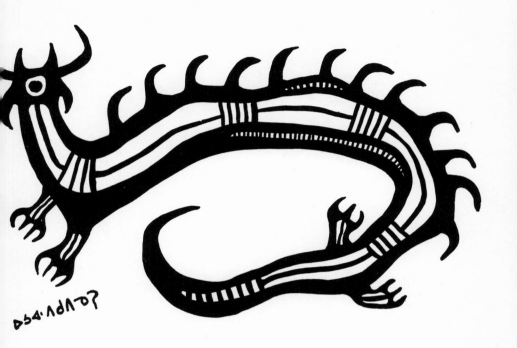

LEGENDS OF MY PEOPLE
THE GREAT OJIBWAY

Illustrated and told by
NORVAL MORRISEAU

Edited by Selwyn Dewdney

McGRAW-HILL RYERSON LIMITED
Toronto   Montreal   New York   London   Sydney
Johannesburg   Mexico   Panama   Düsseldorf
Singapore   Rio de Janeiro   Kuala Lumpur   New Delhi

© The Ryerson Press, 1965

ISBN 0-7700-0110-6

4 5 6 7 8 9 10   JD   10 9 8 7 6 5 4 3 2

PRINTED AND BOUND IN CANADA

TO MY GRANDFATHER
MOSES ("POTAN") NANAKONAGOS

CONTENTS

ILLUSTRATIONS

THE WORLD
OF
NORVAL MORRISEAU

The more adventurous reader will have ignored these pages and may already be staring with some surprise—and perhaps a little awe—at the thunderbird fledglings and their *Eyes blinking light as if it was flashes of Lightning*. For him it will have sufficed that I cleaned out the portages along a route through Morriseau's unfamiliar world that will bring him close to each significant feature of its landscape. Others, however, will reasonably expect some sort of briefing, a map or at least a compass, before they venture so far from home.

The book is based on two manuscripts. One of these I received in the fall of 1960 only three months after meeting the author; the other in 1962. The contents of both were poured out of Morriseau's mind and memory as fast as they rose to the surface without regard for sequence, so that in their original form they comprised a fascinating but often confusing *pot-pourri* of legends, anecdotes, observations, reports and personal comments. The earlier manuscript was the bulkier one. The second was a sort of supplementary issue, rich with new material collected or recollected after the first had been written. There was some repetition of the original stories, which enabled me to choose the fuller account, then round it out with passages or phrases from the other. Sometimes, too, I could add pertinent pieces that I found in Morriseau's letters.

It was no great feat to gather topically related material around the key legends and so form separate chapters of associated lore. The challenge lay in working out a meaningful sequence. Broadly,

viii

the topics grouped themselves into those that echoed the ancient oral tradition and those that more clearly reflected European influence. Of the former no chapter could more appropriately provide the lead than the one containing Morriseau's favourite painting theme—the man that turned into a thunderbird. The next six chapters seemed to fall quite naturally into their present order. This left the Windigo chapter, which offered the perfect bridge from one group to the other. For here the reader would pass from the icy incarnation of an ancient terror to meet Paakuk, grim harbinger of the savage diseases that raced ahead of the invading European. Warfare, too, that had been a minor element in the life of the northern Ojibway, suddenly increased under the pressure of tribal dislocations to the east. Then came actual contact, and whisky; and the book could come to a natural conclusion with the mingling of old and new concepts of the after life, and with the Heaven People, the latest cult to emerge out of underground resistance to the professed faith of the dominant Euro-Canadian culture.

There remained the question of how much "translation" was necessary. For the urgency of the voices emerging out of the shaking tent of Morriseau's world confronted me with an impetuous cursive "printing" that required long familiarity to be read with any ease. In addition, brackets were used for quotation marks, and original spellings like "canio" for canoe were further obscured by opened As, creating an even stranger "cunio." Sometimes whole sentences followed an Ojibway rather than an English word order. I liked the innate respect for the inner man that Professor James Reaney had shown by printing the story of Misshipeshu and the baby in his magazine *Alphabet* without altering so much as a comma. But how many readers would have the interest to see a whole book through, faced with page after page of these puzzling and rarely consistent eccentricities? I decided to compromise by rationalizing the punctuation and correcting misleading spellings. But would this suffice?

The editorial dilemma vanished when Morriseau made it clear that he had no interest in such niceties but was solely concerned that as many readers as possible should become acquainted with what he had written. It is a tribute, however, to the perception and sensitivity of Ryerson's Susan Damania that the formidable task of converting the final text into academically acceptable English was accomplished — like the Nipigon midwife's cure for a difficult delivery—*with No Side Effects whatsoever*. As a concession to the curious who may be unable to locate the December, 1962, issue of *Alphabet*, I have italicized the samples of editorially unadulterated Morriseau that appear in this essay.

A majority, however, will be more interested in the man than in the manuscript. Reading his book and viewing his paintings, they may form their own conclusions about where he is going. It is up to me, nevertheless, to offer some answers to the other essential questions: who is he, and where does he come from?

I first met Norval Morriseau at Red Lake in the summer of 1960, when he was still working in the Cochenour gold mine at the first steady, adequately paid job he had ever had. For me, with a fairly wide acquaintance in the art world, it was startling to be confronted by a man who actually looked like an artist. Everything that the stereotype called for was there: the tall spare figure, the strong elegant hands, the sensitive brooding face. And this was no mere façade. "I have a power in me," he stated with factual dignity as he told me of how he had humbled the Red Lake sorceress.

Certainly there had been a powerful urge to paint his people's folklore. Indeed, the plastic impulse was the basic one, and I doubt whether he would have had the compulsion to write this book had not his faith in the paintings faltered under the patronizing scrutiny of those who bought his early work to hang in their rumpus rooms, as witness this quotation from the transcript of that first interview:

My idea is, why I draw them—see, there's lots of stories that are told in Ojibway. But that wasn't enough for me. I wanted to draw them—that's from my own self—what they would look like. And I never knowed anybody who would be interested. And I thought if they could be some place for a hundred—two hundred—years—not for myself, for my people. Even if I don't get no money I would be glad to paint them just for people to see.

In later conversations he recalled that his first drawings, mostly of conventional subjects, earned him no more than a rap on the knuckles from a harassed teacher, intent on the duller goals of spelling and arithmetic. Back at home, in his late teens the first attempts to portray legendary subjects brought dark looks from friends and relatives who suspected that he was breaking tribal taboos. The first real encouragement he had to paint out of his "own self" was from Joseph Weinstein, the medical officer at Cochenour, who was himself a competent amateur artist, a world traveller and a sophisticated collector of primitive art. In the fall of 1962, independently discovered by Jack Pollock and financially supported that summer by Senator A. Grosart and friends, Morriseau entered the ranks of publicly known Canadian artists with an opening night sell-out at the Pollock Gallery in Toronto.

When I tried to interest a publisher in Morriseau's first manuscript four years ago his art was unknown, and it is fitting that his book should follow rather than precede his recognition as an artist. By his own testimony the oral tradition was not enough. He had to translate it into visual images, and in the process he made it uniquely his own. I can state with some assurance that he owes almost nothing to any external influence; for my own interest in the sources of painting ideas and styles had led me to look fairly thoroughly through Dr. Weinstein's collection of reproductions, to which Morriseau had frequent access, for a style that could have sparked his own. Occasionally a painting subject comes to him in a dream. Even then, however, the painting act is too intuitive and immediate to be the mere illustration of a recollected form.

I put whatever I am Inspired to put, he wrote me at a time when he was trying out plywood as an alternative painting base to his favourite—but persistently warping—birchbark. *I often make some Small drawing Ahead of time what I should Draw. But when I have the plyboard* [in front of me] *I dont Draw what I made in Advance. As I Said I have a feeling I Should Paint what I am Supposed* [intended] *to do. So I Sit. And there my Hand moves and I made a Picture.*

There is nothing mvstical, however, about the Cree syllabics in which the artist renders the Ojibway equivalent of Copper Thunderbird. The forms come from a syllabary invented by the Methodist missionary, John Evans, in the early 1840s, still in wide use today by Cree and Ojibway for trail messages.

The artist, of course, is only one aspect of the man. His writing gives us other glimpses: of a scepticism that wrestles visibly at times with the validity of the old concepts, an earnest desire to be an accurate reporter, a faith in the revelations that come to him in his medicine dreams, and the typically Ojibway humour that will catch the unwary reader off guard, with the bridge built to heaven by the Acme Construction Company. All this, accented by the graphic brilliance of the drawings, confronts us with a mystery when we ask where such a man might come from.

Objectively one might describe the Ojibway families scattered along Highway 11 east of Lake Nipigon as the social and economic backwash of the bush. Whereas a mere two or three generations ago and all through the previous century the adult Ojibway male of the Nipigon country had been essential to a thriving fur trade that gave him an adequate living, he finds today that his bush skills are no longer in demand. Now he must compete in the unskilled labour market, not only with the itinerant unemployed from the cities, but with aggressive young immigrants intent on accumulating the savings from a year or two of bush employment to establish themselves in the cities.

And it is the more ambitious Ojibway who is penalized, for though the government agencies will allow no one to starve, none can prevent a man's relatives from gathering around him when he has a job. So the traditional sharing values of his people—once a major survival factor—now ensure that he will spend his savings after a lay-off long before he finds another job. Those who remain on the Reserve need only follow routine procedures to get groceries when earnings peter out. But those trying to make a go of it outside must often either wait days, or even weeks, before the local credit they need can be arranged, or else subsist on their relatives' government cheques. It takes little imagination to understand what happens to the spirit of an able-bodied man who must turn to his wife's family allowance or to a parent's old age pension for the bread he eats or the beer he drinks. Today no one starves but many are frequently hungry.

To bring the picture closer to the man let me quote from my diary of August 25, 1962: "Up and off to Beardmore, where we found Norval living in a crude summer cabin he had thrown together from the remains of his grandfather's. Norval broke, but expecting money daily" [an advance from Pollock for a new suit and air fare to Toronto] "and looking forward to his Toronto show.

The only food I saw in my eight-hour visit, outside of what I had with me, was a small saucepan of blueberries simmering on an old kitchen wood range that stood in the centre of the clearing. The passive way in which this situation was accepted remains incomprehensible unless we relate it to two facts: one the absence in the area of any jobs; the other an age-old attitude, learned through millenia of survival in a harsh environment. In the old days when blizzards blew or game disappeared it was wise to conserve food and energy and sit it out until the break came. Now they were still sitting it out but more securely than in ancient times: for they knew that Norval's cheque was on its way. There was no sign of impatience in the interval; talking with them, one would think they had not a worry in the world.

Morriseau, who now has a wife and four children of his own to feed, expressed this attitude beautifully for me in a letter he wrote last winter:

Lets put it this way. I know what it is to be Hungry and Poor in Cloths. But the Spirit of one that is poor Shall never be weaken by Hunger, as Hunger is a Good matter. This is what gives a man Life and Wisdom. I dont Regret that I was Hungery.

Nor did anyone in this little settlement, cleared out of the second-growth jack pine that bordered the Beardmore garbage dump, complain about there being only one backhouse for the twenty people living in three small cabins. And even if there was no plumbing of any kind, there was plenty of water to be had merely by walking to the lakeshore eighty yards or so on the other side of the highway and dipping a pail in the lake. For light at night there was a single gasoline lamp minus chimney and fuel. But that was no problem either. One could go to bed when it got dark, or stroll over to town where electric lights glowed in the beer parlour. A little beer went a long way on an empty stomach. At one end of the clearing sat an ancient Chevrolet that the artist's half-brother had used the previous summer in commuting to and from a good, but temporary job fifty miles

xiv

down the highway. All four tires were flat; one from a deliberate axe cut.

Add to this unpromising physical background the young Ojibway's educational handicaps. Picture the bewilderment of the beginner trying to understand a teacher who cannot speak his language and has no special training to deal with the situation. Follow the seasonal migrations of his family and ask about his school attendance. In fact, the only consistent schooling young Norval had were the two years he boarded at the Indian Residential School in Fort William. So it is not too surprising to learn that when he finally left school to help maintain his family's subsistence standards he had achieved no more than a Grade IV standing. His post-graduate work was done mostly in the village dump where he eased a little the itch of an enquiring mind by delving among the discarded magazines and books he found there. In his twenties he became an authority, by empirical research, on malnutrition and chronic unemployment, and gained some insight into pulmonary infections during a year in the tuberculosis sanitarium in Fort William. Of this decade he writes, *Lets leave it void—too much Involved.*

Such a schooling only increases the mystery. But Morriseau supplies a major clue: his grandfather. The only name he entered in a genealogy form I sent him to fill in was that of his mother's father, Moses Nanakonagos. *It is only his name I want to mention,* he wrote below, *so that in one way the other his Good heart, his good Teachings etc Shall be Repayed.* Of his actual father he saw little; the grandfather took on that parent's role. *I knewed he was not my father,* he told me in a letter, [but] *I began to Love and Respect him more and more as he advanced in years, as this was all a Part of me and I must Carry on his Wisdom.*

On my second visit to Beardmore I was lucky enough to glimpse the warmth and humour of the bond betwen the young man and the old one. During our three-way conversation in English they made asides to each other in Ojibway that, for all I knew, were poking fun at me. Whatever the topic, it was obviously a mere vehicle for the wit and repartee that flowed between them, each adding a further touch to the other's quips until both would break out in a climax of hilarity.

Out of this intimacy came a kind of education that is vouchsafed to few. Emerging at sunrise from his cabin on Sand Point Reserve, the dark-eyed child searched the mists that wraithed the reaches of Lake Nipigon, yearning to sight one of the huge birds that might at that very moment be hunting horned snakes out there. Were there young thunderbirds now in the great stone nest at the summit of the hill above the cabin, the nest that no man had seen? Last night, lying on the rough cabin floor that was his bed, he had listened to the soft cadences of his native tongue as his grandfather told him how the mysterious Maymay-gwaysiwuk, with their strange hairy noseless faces, would emerge from their home in the living rock, paddling their stone canoe. In winter, as man and boy stopped on the trap-line trail to boil a pail of tea, the lad would beg for another story about Wesuhkaychauk (in English, "Whisky Jack"). So Moses would begin, gesturing and posturing with droll mimicry as he warmed to the bright expectancy of the lad's eyes, until the mischievous shaman-hero of their people came alive, and the tea grew cold. And later, with the snow creaking under young Norval's snowshoes and frostbite numbing the skin of his face, he might cast a nervous glance backward, fancying he had heard the paralyzing shout of the Windigo from across the ice of a distant lake.

Yet even so remarkable a grandfather merely pushes the mystery back two generations; and we must ask what manner of people his forebears were, three centuries ago, when the first *coureurs de bois* portaged past Virgin Falls and pushed their canoes into the water of Lake Nipigon. Failing any

xvi

answer, we turn again to their living descendants. Have these people, stripped of all that they were, preserved some quality that could produce the magic of a Morriseau?

On my first visit to the west shore of Lake Nipigon I met blue-eyed, heavily bearded men who pronounced their French names with an English accent but spoke only their native language, Ojibway. Had I asked anyone on the Reserve whether the face hair or lack of skin colour had affected his feelings about them, he would have taken me for an idiot. In my own wanderings I have found the Cree and Ojibway completely free of this kind of bias. And though they conceal a deep resentment towards the powers that be, yet they are incapable of transferring this hostility to any half-decent agent of these same powers. Sometimes when a "white" man has unpredictably "gone native," it is explained in terms of the sexual permissiveness of the culture. In my opinion, however, this is only a minor feature of the broad spectrum of acceptance one finds in Ojibway society. It is the total climate of tolerance that exerts such a powerful appeal to all who experience it. I am sure, for example, that it was not the limited sexual attractions of Ojibway life that led a mutual friend of Morriseau's and mine, born and bred in Toronto of Anglo-Saxon stock, with security and a promising career ahead of him in a provincial service, to abandon these prospects, his wife and children and become *de facto* an "Indian."

How has it been possible for these people, even after the disappearance of their material culture, to maintain their resistance to the values of an impinging culture with a passive power that baffles and bewilders every integrating agency of church, state and industry? Could it be that Morriseau, measuring our materialistically oriented society against the background of his own people's spiritual values, has had good reason to take pride and reassurance from his Ojibway identity?

The more numerous part of the Ojibway people lived north and west of Lake Superior, but retained their contact with the southern bands until the United States began to administer its territory along the newly established boundary with British North America. A substantial literature records the legends, beliefs and practices of the southern Ojibway, but records of the northern bands are scanty and confusing. The British take-over that followed the original French penetration created a babel of tribal names that plague scholars to this day. The rough tactics of rival fur companies discouraged private travellers. Throughout the nineteenth century Christian missionaries were so hostile to native beliefs that "pagan" terms were often omitted from the dictionaries they compiled, and each denomination devised its own phonetical system for spelling Ojibway words. Early in the 1900s spellings froze while a system prevailed that spelled "way" as *wa*, and "wah" as *wau*. But this has been forgotten, so that Torontonians blissfully insist that *Keewatin*, the name of one of their streets and Ojibway for "north wind," should be pronounced Kee*wah*tin!

The French first met the Ojibway at Sault Ste. Marie and called them *Saulteaux*. Today this name, frequently anglicized as "Soto," is official for a few bands of Ojibway in southeastern Manitoba, among whom the French language lingered longest in the west. La Vérendrye's guide called the people living in this area *Cristanois*, which came to be applied, in the form of *Kristenaux*, to neighbours farther north and west, later simplified by the English into "Cree." Only recently it has been established that bands in northwestern Ontario, until then designated as Cree, actually spoke Ojibway. In the seventeenth and eighteenth centuries the Siouan-speaking Assiniboines (Ojibway *Ahsin* for "stone," hence sometimes called Stonies) were being pushed out of Ontario by the western Ojibway. Morriseau's *Noduweck* in the Little Grouse stories (the ending is the Ojibway plural) and

Alexander Mackenzie's *Nadowasis* (English plural) have their French variant in *Nadouessioux* (French plural) from which the surviving name, Sioux, was derived. But the original Ojibway word signified a poisonous snake, that is, enemy, and was applied to any hostile group, such as the Sioux in the west or the Iroquois in the east. Since the latter were Longhouse People, the same tag could easily get stuck on the former. And I add, merely to cap this confusion, the fact that the *Otchipwé* (a French spelling) frequently prefer to call themselves *Ahnishinahbag*!

Whatever name we wish to use, the simple fact is that throughout historic times the people in question have occupied the watershed of Lake Superior and the region westward to Lake Winnipeg. They speak a dialect of the Algonkian tongue, the most widespread aboriginal language on the continent. Their culture was shared, with regional variations, by all the inhabitants of the Canadian Shield Woodlands, from the Woods Cree of northern Saskatchewan to the Montagnais of the St. Lawrence north shore. The shaking tent rites described by Morriseau in these pages are still practised in the Rainy Lake district of Ontario, and have been reported throughout the southern Shield since early historic times. The mysterious Maymaygwaysiwuk, too, were widely believed in.

George Quimby's *Indian Life in the Great Lakes* offers a lucid account of what is so far known, or deduced, from the archaeology of the region. The historic Ojibway either inherited or assimilated the Woodland cultures that prevailed from 500 B.C. until the European intrusion. Preceding that, a Boreal Archaic culture took form some seven thousand years ago. Cultural affinities with the early peoples of northern Europe and Asia lead some scholars to believe that there was once a "circumpolar culture" through all the Boreal forests of the northern hemisphere. Bear cults on all three continents are cited as part of the evidence. If the sacred bear beliefs that

Morriseau describes are echoes of these Boreal Archaic ones they are old indeed. J. G. Kohl, whose *Kitchi-Gami* describes the south shore Ojibway of the 1850s, reported the peculiar reverence of these bands for lumps of native copper, which one is tempted to relate to the Old Copper culture that prevailed around Lake Superior coincidentally with the Boreal Archaic. Whether or not there is any connection, the awe in which the metal was held does account for the formidableness with which the name Copper Thunderbird strikes Ojibway ears.

There is evidence that the isolated cultures of the Boreal forests maintained themselves unchanged for incredibly long periods, each generation handing on the oral tradition and magic rites with painstaking accuracy. It is far otherwise, however, when one culture impinges on another. When Christianity arrived, with a superior technology to enhance its prestige, it made a major impact on native beliefs, throwing some into confusion, driving others underground, and stimulating new cults with native messiahs to champion them. On top of that, tribal losses from the new epidemics and increased warfare promoted intertribal fusions and the wholesale adoption of captives that accelerated cultural diffusion.

The extent of such acculturation will cause some to challenge Morriseau's claim to have "the proper version of this lore." But this is to misunderstand his claim. As he himself points out in the stories of Little Grouse, Ojibway beliefs could have been influenced by the adoption of Assiniboine captives; and he frequently reminds us that his one concern is to reproduce the oral tradition as it has been related to him. My own search for folklore related to aboriginal rock art in the Shield country, that has involved me in interviews with scores of Cree and Ojibway over the past eight years, leaves me with two impressions: how amazingly similar some stories are that I have picked up as far apart as Lake Nipissing and Lac la Ronge, and yet how many variations and even contradictions I can get from informants in the same community. So the confusion of concepts we encounter in Morriseau's collection faithfully reflects the ethnological facts.

One final point I would like to make before the reader puts this briefing behind him, and I speak out of some insight acquired by a look into the wells of my own prejudice. It will be all too easy for some to bring to this book the posture of amused condescension that we of the Anglo-Saxon tradition too easily assume. Too often, I suspect, a real contempt lurks behind the mask of our self-advertised tolerance. Such will see no more here than a collection of superstitious rubbish. At the other extreme, I am reminded of the sentimental thousands a mere generation ago who read the books of Grey Owl without an inkling that the emerging image of a "noble red man" was their own wishful projection, shared and exploited by one of themselves, who as an English lad called Archie Belaney dreamed of being an "Indian" when he grew up, and made his dream come true. For my part, Norval Morriseau is neither a "bush bum," nor a picturesque aborigine. This is a sensitive, unusually intelligent human being, faced with the agonizing problem of integrating within his own person the conflicting elements of two deeply dissimilar cultures. Sometimes he can cope with the moods of black despair that this dichotomy brings on by taking long walks in the bush. Sometimes it drives him to drink, to achieve the temporary but real relief that is, perhaps, our most significant gift to his people.

If one has an Intelgent mind he Could Live Side by Side with our Ancient ways, and Same time get us where we Should be.

Is this merely a romantic dream? Is the swift erosion of minority cultures now going on around the globe an inevitable, irreversible process? Is our Canadian vision of nurturing diverse but equal cultural identities within the larger context of a distinctive national one mere sentimental nonsense?

Or are we ignoring deeper, tougher realities to our future peril?

For me, all these questions come to focus in the person of Norval Morriseau. Now let him speak, for himself and for his people.

SELWYN DEWDNEY

MY NAME
IS
COPPER
THUNDERBIRD

In these pages will be found the beliefs, the tales and legends up to the present day, of the great Ojibway nation of Lake Nipigon and the Thunder Bay district. This book is written in honour of my great Ojibway Indian ancestors who roamed the Great Lakes for centuries upon centuries and their descendants who live today all over Ontario.

I am Norval Morriseau and my Indian name is Copper Thunderbird. I am a born artist. A few people are born artists and most others are not, and it is the same with the Indians. I have grown up with many stories and legends of my people, the great Ojibway Indians, and I have made paintings of these legends, although very few people have yet seen them. I believe each painting would be worth exhibiting in a gallery. Each one illustrates an Ojibway legend as purely uncorrupted as a modern-day Indian could possibly paint. I am not sure if the art itself would be accepted as original Indian art, but painters are rarely found among the Ojibway. The Department of Indian Affairs at one time wanted to give me art lessons but in my opinion this would have spoilt me, as nobody else could teach me the kind of paintings I do and perhaps I would have learned something else to corrupt my style.

I had reached only Grade Four on quitting school, which I regret now, but I have read a lot to improve my education. I speak English well and many times have been told by my friends that

I know how to hold a good conversation and must have had a good school education. Over the years I became an avid student of my people, the great Ojibway. I have as much interest in their history and lore as any anthropologist and have studied all I can. I believe I have the proper version of this lore; I have lived among my people all my life and, being an Indian, I was readily told anything I wanted to know just for the asking. Also I do not pick these stories and legends from any book, as such books are not to be found anywhere.

I understand a lot is known of other respected tribes of North American Indians but only a little of the great Ojibway people. I believe it will require some years of study before much is known of my people. I wish to see this accomplished in my lifetime, so I am writing this book as a foundation and I am sure many more will follow.

I wish some of the educated Ojibway Indians would take the same interest in our history as I have always done. My people, be proud of your great culture that was once mighty, your great societies, the Midaywewin and Wabinowin, and the great Ojibway Medicine Society of the Three Fires.

Today we wonder, and are distracted by the effects of the white man's ways that we cannot cope with. Those of us who are lucky have made it, but many of us are still behind because we are trying to live like our white brothers and by their religion, ignoring our great ancestral cultures. If we are intelligent about this, we could live side by side with our ancient ways and at the same time get where we should be, like our white brothers. We are helped in order to help ourselves and it is now up to us to try from there.

Remember we have accomplished a lot within a hundred years. A hundred years ago we lived off the land by hunting and trapping. Today we do not. We have been to school and learned the ways of the white man's world. In another hundred years from today we will be mixed with our great country into the Canadian way of life. How will we benefit by knowing that way of life if we set aside our ancestral rites and beliefs?

I feel as I am writing this book that it would indeed be a great loss if these legends and beliefs of my people, the Ojibway, are forgotten. For so much is lost. Every day an Ojibway elder dies and every day some of the knowledge of his ancestors dies with him. Only after he is dead is it realized how great that loss is. Also some Ojibway do not pass on their beliefs for fear of some misfortune, or they wait until the day comes to die and then it is too late.

We, therefore, must write down and record legends, art, songs and beliefs, not for ourselves alone but for all future Ojibway. One would not like to open a book to read that we were tough, ignorant savages or a bunch of drunkards, but rather a people who were proud of their great culture.

N. M.

THE
THUNDERBIRD
BELIEFS

The Ojibway believed the thunder to be a great massive bird called a thunderbird, whose eyes shoot out lightning and thunder. The first thunder in early spring was something good to hear, for the Ojibway welcomed their protector again from its home in the south where it had been all the winter. Offerings of tobacco were placed on the ground or on water or put into the stove to burn, or sacred pipes were smoked by the elders to the thunderbird in the early spring.

It is known among the Ojibway that the thunderbirds had a huge nest on the mountains of the earth and large blankets of clouds were always seen to cover the nest. Although the thunderbird was never seen to come and go from its nest, it was known to be there. Lightning and thunder were heard only at these places. At Lake Nipigon in the olden times there was a mountain across the old Sand Point Indian Reserve where the thunderbirds had a nest made of stones that was always seen by the Ojibway. No one ever went to find out what was really up there but Indians did not need to find out, for the Ojibway knew it was the thunderbird and considered that place sacred. About thirty years before the coming of the white man into that area of Lake Nipigon the blanket of clouds seen at the mountain began to lift and moved away forever, and the Ojibway saw a huge nest. Later that summer the thunderbirds destroyed every trace of the place and pretty nearly levelled half the mountain in order to leave no evidence.

I was told that the thunderbirds were believed

4

to have a great nest on one of the mountains by Lake Superior. Some eighty-five years ago two young boys started to climb this mountain to find out if a thunderbird really was there although they had been told never to go up that mountain. When they got to the top they saw two big newly hatched birds who were still hairy and whose eyes blinked light like flashes of lightning. The frightened boys ran down the hill and told what they had seen. An Indian who in his youth had seen these boys died at Heron Bay some years ago. Later this same story was told me by a relative who said that the birds moved away, where it is not known. Huge stone nests of these majestic birds are still seen in some parts of Ontario. One is located in Manitoba, another in the Deer Lake area in the wilderness north of Red Lake.

One Ojibway elder was believed to be a special messenger of the Great Spirit. This Indian lived at Virgin Falls at the mouth of Lake Nipigon. He told the Ojibway that God sent him to earth in company with two other people whose names were Stone and Water. This man of honour said that one day Lake Nipigon would be flooded, the Nipigon River would flow into Lake Nipigon again and Virgin Falls would be lost forever in the water. The Ojibway at that time did not believe this man, although he was respected for his great medicine drums. Fifty years later this fine portage was flooded by a hydro dam. The pressure forced the river to flow backwards into Lake Nipigon, and his words came true. How he knew this would take place is a mystery. Some Indians who heard this old man say these words are still alive to see them coming true.

Where did the white man get his electric power from—the thunderbirds? This is a general belief among the Ojibway. "At one time," said this same Ojibway elder, "I went west and came upon some white men making a golden serpent that was hollow inside. About an hour after the serpent was put out in the prairies, thunderclouds were seen to come over in its direction. This snake was made so that the thunderbirds would be attracted to it and have some lightning caught inside the hollow part." When the thunderbirds saw the serpent they dropped from the heavens showers of lightning. Some of it got caught inside the hollow part and when there was enough the white man took the lightning and made it into electric power. The Ojibway elder also said that one time the white men took off for the thunderclouds on a plane and when they got up there they shot at the thunderbirds, took only the heads, put them in huge pots and the juice of the heads was turned into electric power.

The Ojibway of the Lake Nipigon area believed in two kinds of thunderbirds, one had the ordinary bill, or beak, the other had a long, crooked beak. The latter the Ojibway believed had a very bad temper, made the loudest noise and destroyed Indians by lightning, but the other was of a mild temper and did not make very much noise and these are the ones we generally hear. There is also the thunderbird who is alone and has a lot of power. The Ojibway have a legend based on this lone thunderbird, called *The Indian that Became a Thunderbird.*

Once in ancient times there lived seven North American Indian brothers. According to this legend these seven brothers had never seen a woman before. How each was born without both parents this legend does not mention. One day the youngest of the seven whose name was Wahbi Ahmik, White Beaver, went hunting in the great forest. There he met Nimkey Banasik, Thunderbird Woman. White Beaver was not afraid for he was glad to see such a beautiful woman. The young warrior took his lady fair to his wigwam where they lived together as man and wife and were very happy. All his brothers liked her except Ahsin, Stone, the oldest brother, who hated her but tried not to show his feelings. One day White

6

Beaver went hunting and was very happy thinking of all the blessings he was given. It was on this day that Ahsin's hate became too much for him to bear.

When White Beaver returned from the hunt he discovered bloodstains around the campfire and near his wigwam. He then rushed into his tent and, not seeing his woman Nimkey Banasik anywhere, his anger grew against his brother Stone because now White Beaver knew that it must have been Stone who hated his wife so much that he killed her.

White Beaver rushed to the tent of Ahsin and said, "I know you hated her, but what wrong did she do to you? It must indeed have been a great wrong. Tell me, Ahsin, what have you done, for I see her blood on the ground leading into the forest?"

Ahsin was not afraid of his brother's anger and replied, "You brought this woman Nimkey Banasik to your wigwam and to my presence when I hate the sight of a woman. I hated her the first time I saw her. We were all happy together before she came, so I planned to get rid of her for good. When you left this morning I saw Nimkey Banasik by the fireside preparing moose meat and cooking for you. I got my sharpest arrow and placed it in my bow. The arrow found its mark in the hip of this woman I hated. After I shot the arrow she jumped up and half ran into the forest, and loud noises of thunder were heard up in the heavens. I was afraid of the thunder and I was afraid to follow her to make sure I had killed her."

Wahbi Ahmik asked Stone, Ahsin, "Where were my other brothers at the time this took place and why did they not stop you from doing what you did?" Stone answered, "I sent them away. As you see, none have returned yet."

"Now my brother Stone," replied White Beaver, "I am indeed mad enough to kill you, even if you are my blood brother. You are a very foolish man and very evil. Even though I am mad at you, still

7

in a way I am sorry for you. My brother Stone, tell me, did it ever come to your mind what or who Nimkey Banasik was ? Could you not think what her name meant—Great Thunderbird Woman? I had meant to tell you but I did not do so right away because I knew you did not like her. This woman could have been the one to boost future generations, if her blood and ours had been mixed together by means of a child. For this woman was a thunderbird in human form. Nimkey Banasik had six sisters. With them we could have founded a great civilization. Now it is too late. And from this day forward Indians to come, from generation to generation, will know that it was you who stopped that progress. But there will be Indians coming from the east whose women our brothers will marry. As for me, I am leaving, never to return until I find this woman, for I shall follow her. I have a feeling that she is still alive, for she had a lot of power."

Then White Beaver followed the trail that led into the forest, over valleys and mountains and far into the great forest, until he reached a huge mountain whose top reached over the very clouds and beyond. He started to climb until the earth could not be seen any more, for now he had reached the very top. There on a blanket of clouds stood a great majestic wigwam that shot forth thunder and lightning bolts. From the wigwam was heard the laughter of many women. All at once it stopped, for his presence was felt. As the wigwam flap opened, there stood Nimkey Banasik looking beautiful as ever, with no sign of blood or of the arrow. She said, "Why did you follow me?"

"I came because you are my life."

Then the woman said, "Come forward. We will give you power to walk on the clouds. Come inside, I want you to meet my parents."

Inside the wigwam were seated two old thunderbirds in human form. Each looked full of power and wisdom. In their eyes he saw light flashing

8

The Thunderbird—Destroyer and Restorer

off and on. The Indian was very hungry. The old man said, "What shall we give this Indian? I know he will not eat as we do, for we are of a different nature and we cannot keep him in heaven too long."

So the Indian was asked by the thunderbird sister what he would eat. The Indian said, "I eat moose and deer."

"We will try to obtain some for you."

A big roar of thunder was heard. From the human form the thunderbirds changed into their natural state and flew away. About half an hour later they brought back a big horned snake with two heads and three tails. It was offered to Wahbi Ahmik to eat, but he was unable to do so. Even looking at it made him sick. But each morning he grew more hungry. Again he was asked if he would like something to eat. Two more trips were made but proved unsuccessful. The second time he was offered a snake sturgeon, the third a great big cat demigod. He refused all, as White Beaver could not eat in the same manner as the thunderbirds.

Finally the old woman said to her older daughter, "I am aged in wisdom. I have great knowledge. I know you like this human who is an Indian. As you see, even if he were to be one of us he could not eat as we do. Take him to your great medicine thunderbird uncle, known as Southern Medicine Thunderbird, who lives in the south. Among the thunderbirds there I am sure he will have medicine for this Indian."

White Beaver was laid in a big blanket of cloud that reminded him of a rabbit-skin blanket and he was taken in that manner to the far south. This blanket also covered him, so that he should not look. Before leaving there was a great flash and White Beaver heard thunder and then felt the cloud moving. After some time everything stopped and he was told to get up. As he looked around a big medicine lodge was seen in the middle of a great cloud. Below, on the second layer of clouds,

were seen many lodges and wigwams of thunderbirds of many different kinds, who all had human
forms. As they entered the medicine lodge Nimkey
Banasik spoke to her uncle and said, "My mother,
your sister, sent us to try to give medicine to this
Indian so that he may eat as we do and if possible
become one of us."

For a while the medicine thunderbird stood in
silence, then said, "All right, let it be known to
this Indian that if he will take the medicine I
shall give he will never return to earth but will
become a thunderbird, to live up in the heavens
for ever." Then the medicine thunderbird took
out two small medicine eggs coloured light blue,
mixed them together in a small pot and advised
Ahmik to drink the first drink.

When White Beaver took it he felt that some
power had entered him, and as he looked at his
feet he noticed they were those of a thunderbird.
At the next drink, the whole amount, he changed
into a thunderbird. His human form, the wigwams, the medicine lodge, all had disappeared.
Everyone was now a thunderbird. So, being hungry, he flew onward to the home of the female
thunderbirds and feasted on the very things he
could not eat some short time ago.

But the Indians that lived below remembered
this Indian who became a thunderbird. Ahsin's
disgrace was known, and the women of the people
who came from the east married some of the
brothers, and so on from generation to generation
until this modern era. This legend is respected
among my people. Ojibway belief states that this
thunderbird is still heard up in the great heavens
and I myself have heard it twice in my lifetime.

The following legend was told to me. Once an
Ojibway baby dreamed that a giant bird, a big
eagle, grabbed him and flew with him toward a
huge, high mountain that had a flat surface. The
big eagle left the baby there. Later it would return
to devour the child. The child started to cry in

12

his dream and a great thunderbird came out of the skies to help him, and it grabbed the baby with forked lightning and took him from the ground and left him on a great plain, or desert. There the thunderbird spoke to the baby and said, "I will help you only once. So take care, for this will repeat itself in real life." From there the baby travelled home and by the time he reached his own place where he was born he was old. Then the baby woke up.

As he grew into a boy and into a man this dream planted upon his mind a great solid mark of fear. He was always on the look-out for that big eagle. One day this dream came true, as told in a legend of a huge bird that flew a man to a warm country, perhaps the American southeast, or Florida.

One clear, early winter day this Indian was on the ice spearing fish through a hole. As he bent down to look into the hole a wind was heard up above. Looking up he saw a big bird, called Keebonesee, like a huge eagle with enormous claws and a great wing-spread. The Indian could not run any place as the huge bird was about to grab him. With his spear in his hand he was taken up into the air, so far up that the earth was a blur. Finally after flying up in a circle the bird started going straight.

The Indian travelled for some time. Then he noticed the air became hotter. Then he saw mountains and upon the rocks was a huge nest built of big pieces of wood, where the Indian noticed the bones of different animals. The bird made a circle and tried to kill the Indian by hurling him three times against the walls of the huge rocks. His spear prevented this in some way. Finally the bird was either tired or gave up hope of killing him and dropped the Indian into the nest.

As he landed he saw a cave. There he lived for some time. Each day the huge bird would bring back some animal and the Indian ate what was left over. The rocks, or cliff, were very steep and there was no way to go down. The Indian lived each day in hope that one day he would escape. To jump would mean death. Clouds and mist were always there. The mountains were very high and the earth, or tree line, was seen down below in the great far distance.

It cannot be said how long this Indian stayed up there in that lonely cave. One day he noticed the bird brought its mate and began to add more wood and build the huge nest bigger. One morning after this the Indian saw two huge eggs, and again one morning there were newly hatched birds. Hope was in his mind. Now there was a way to escape.

He planned to wait until the young birds grew a little bigger, then he would kill one, take its wings and tie them stretched against his own arms and jump. In this manner he thought that the weight of his body would fall more slowly than if he jumped without them. He succeeded. It took time to jump from one place to another until he set foot on solid ground. Looking up, the Indian saw the two birds flying around making a great noise, perhaps because of his presence or because of the loss of their offspring. Anyway, the Indian headed for the bush, although it was strange to him.

Finally through a medicine dream he started on his journey back home to Ontario. Through many plains and wooded areas and after many hardships he finally reached the place he had left so many moons ago when he was young. By that time he was old and no one was left who knew him. That is all.

OJIBWAY BELIEFS
ABOUT NATURE,
WEATHER
AND OTHER
DIFFERENT MATTERS

The Ojibway believe the earth to be their mother and that we are children of the earth. The sun is the sister of the world, the moon is the brother. The sky, water, fire and stone are also closely related to the earth. The figure on the moon is believed to be that of a small boy carrying two water pails. At one time a young Ojibway boy about ten years old was told not to look at the moon too long for it was forbidden and the moon would take him away, but the lad, who had two water pails with him to get water, wanted to prove if this were true and kept on staring. Finally the moon came closer and closer and took away the Ojibway lad and this is where he has lived from that day. The Ojibway children are told not to look at the moon too long and often ask their elders why there is a boy with two pails on the moon, and this is the story that is told to them.

The great medicine spider appeared to the Ojibway centuries ago to teach them to make a net of hide string in the same manner as the spider makes his web, to protect them from sorcery. It is believed that if a sorcerer comes to harm the owner of the sacred net his spirit body, or dream body, will be caught like a fly in this net and be devoured by the spider, and if that spirit body is caught his real body, including his spirit body, will die. Today these sacred nets can still be seen among the

Ojibway, made out of fine thread with small rattles tied on both sides.

To kill frogs means rain, and it is forbidden to kill frogs and turtles for fear of angering the frog spirit. Indians used frogs and turtles with sorcery to bring upon earth much-needed rains.

Killing a snake was not allowed because of its relationship and resemblance to the medicine snake, although it is smaller. But if a snake is killed it must not be laid on its back to show its belly to the sky, because this angers the thunder-birds and foretells a thunderstorm, when they would cast lightning upon the snake.

One day I was with my brother in Dorion Township, Ontario, at Good-Morning Lake. We got up very early, about four o'clock in the morning, while it was cold outside. My brother Frank shot at a nighthawk that was flying around in the air and it finally landed in a clearing. Sure enough, he killed it.

We travelled until six that morning and pretty nearly got lost because a thick fog came down that lasted until twelve that day when it finally lifted.

Later that afternoon I began to wonder what would cause the fog to fall so heavily on us. Then I remembered and told my brother that I had heard a story of two Indian children who found a nighthawks' nest on a rock and poked a stick at them, and it began to get foggy and rained.

Indian legend states fog is the clothing of the thunderbird, or a blind that he uses not to be seen. If a fog is very thick it is believed that the thunderbird comes down to earth to eat the evil serpents. Was it because we killed this hawk that its spirit form cried to its relation, the thunder-bird, in return to send a fog upon us? I do not know. But my brother never tried to kill another for fear of the fog descending upon him. Other Ojibway told me the same. Some say it begins to thunder, storm and rain. Anyway, this is a belief to be held with respect.

16

Beaver and Wigwam (Representing Human Life)

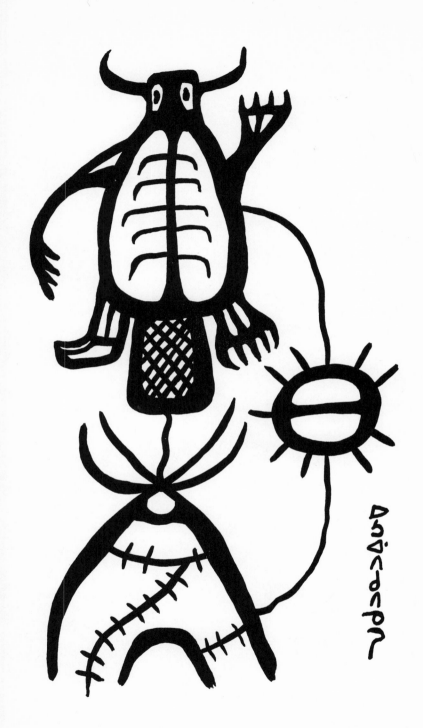

The Ojibway Indians at Lake Nipigon had what we call the stone medicine that was picked up from the earth itself. There are many legends of the origin of these sacred sands and stone medicines. The Indians called this matter onaman. The red onaman sand, which is the colour of darkish blood found in iron rust, has a legend that tells how at one time when the world was young there lived a huge beaver in a great pond. Maybe the pond was Lake Superior. One day when the great beaver came to the top of the water the thunderbirds were up above. A thunderbird, known as the hunger bird, saw this beaver and came swooping down and seized it and flew up into the air to feast on its flesh. The claws of the thunderbird went deep into the beaver's hide and flesh. From the beaver's wounds sprang blood that fell all over the earth. From that blood was formed the sacred medicine sand called onaman.

The great Ojibway used this for charms to bring them more luck in hunting and trapping. They would make a medicine bag by putting the onaman sand of the beaver's blood into a deer-hide bag and tying to it three eagle feathers, one from each wing and one from the tail, to represent the hunter bird.

In all the lakes where rock paintings are found the Ojibway put sacred signs on the face of the cliffs. I was told by my grandfather that the sacred markings we see on the cliff walls were put there by the power of the Indian who executed them, that he did not use any sacred onaman sand as was claimed, but his actual fingers. From the fingers sprang out red matter that was so powerful and so sacred that it will remain always without fading. Other markings that have faded were made by onaman sand.

It is believed by my people that these rock paintings did not foretell or leave any information, but were sacred signs meaning little to anyone outside that area. To those who lived there, however, they would mean something. The Indians might even have known the painter and been told the meanings, although after a hundred years these would be lost because the men who knew had died during that time without telling anyone else.

The Ojibway have many legends and stories of a demigod named Nanabojou. One story tells how he had ten wives, another how he pretended to have died in order to marry his older daughter, yet another how he tied himself to the feet of the mighty geese and flew up with them into the air, later to fall into a toilet. Nanabojou called all the wolves his blood brothers and there are many more tales about him, all different. Some believe he was like the Bible Noah.

Ojibway have a firm belief in the great Flood as related in the Bible, but there is an Indian version that tells how the water gods were mad because Nanabojou had killed a frog that was a medicine-man. He skinned the frog, put on its skin and went to the lodges of the water gods. When he got there, on the floor was the great water god Misshipeshu badly wounded and in pain. Nanabojou was welcome; for the water gods, thinking it was the frog medicine-man, did not know it was Nanabojou in the frog skin. The water god had an arrow inside him and the "frog" was told to take it out. Instead of pulling the arrow out, he pushed it in farther until the water god died. At the door was Nanabojou's blood brother the wolf, who grabbed the skin and ran into the forest. Later the water gods found that it was really Nanabojou. This made them mad and they put a flood upon the earth. Nanabojou felt sorry for the animals and made a huge raft to save them all.

I cannot and will not believe that Nanabojou, the chief demigod, was a rabbit, nor will the Ojibway. One who was intelligent above all life could not have been the meek and lowly rabbit. Our belief at Lake Nipigon is that he was a man, a demigod by rights who took human form. A legend is told how Nanabojou centuries ago burned his rectum, because his rectum did not speak to him to give warning. Would a rabbit have the intelligence to do this? Also legend states that all the wolves were Nanabojou's brothers. Then it must have been a sight to see a rabbit leading a pack of wolves as brothers. And it would be an insult to this great Ojibway legendary demigod to say he looked like a man with long rabbit-ears. This is not the real legend, but is of white origin. The Ojibway belief is the one to go by, that Nanabojou looked like an Indian, not a rabbit. This does not mean to say that all demigods looked like humans.

The beaver was considered sacred by the Ojibway who, because of its meat and fur, regarded it as the source of life. No Ojibway will ever throw beaver bones to a dog. If he does it is considered to bring bad luck and he would never catch beaver again for a period of some years. It is believed by the Ojibway that the dog bites the bones harder than a human and the beaver feels it if a dog chews his bones. The kneecaps of the beaver are taken right away as it is skinned and are put in the fire or the water where no dog can get them. Beaver meat also is never given to a dog to eat although traps for wild animals are baited with beaver meat, but no harm comes of this.

The first beaver of the year that is caught by the Ojibway is always eaten in a manner that is considered sacred. Some Indians would spread a clean cloth and have the first beaver eaten on the floor, not on the table. All the bones are tied in a bundle in a clean cloth with ribbons and tobacco and are thrown in the water. This is believed to bring good luck in catching beaver for the coming season.

THE OJIBWAY WATER BEINGS AND DEMIGODS OF THE NIPIGON AREA

The Ojibway of this area believe that there is a huge red sturgeon in the waters of Lake Nipigon who has eyes that shine like the sun and who is known among the Ojibway as the keeper of all the offering rocks in the Lake Nipigon area.

There is an underwater grave, or tunnel, leading from Nipigon Bay into Lake Nipigon and to all the offering rocks of that area. Indians had medicine dreams concerning these tunnels and it is claimed by the Ojibway that there was one Indian who once saw these tunnels through the power of a lake-dweller, or merman, at Poplar Lodge at Lake Nipigon. Indians were spearing fish by torchlight when one Ojibway noticed at the bottom of the gravel a merman. Not knowing that it was a merman but figuring it was a fish, he threw his spear at it. The water began to churn and his hands were stuck to the handle of the spear until he was pulled, body and all, into the water. He did not drown, but felt some power being forced into his body to enable him to breathe; then he was taken for a journey to all the water caves and tunnels, to all the offering rocks at Lake Nipigon, at Ombabika Bay, Gull Bay and Orient Bay. The mermen spoke to him and said, "We want you to be our representative. We want you to erect offering rocks wherever we have taken you and to tell the Ojibway about these tunnels."

The mermen brought good luck to those who offered them tobacco and, in return, helped the Indians to travel safely on all lakes and rivers by

Maymaygwaysiwuk

making the waters calm. Of course the Ojibway Indians of the whole Nipigon area saw these beings in person, for each one looked like a human but with rather a funnily shaped nose and face; they were very shy and seemed to hide their faces in shame. Ojibway Indians, however, always told them not to be afraid, for they were very respected. And the water beings knew this through mind-readings. Of course no water being was ever worshipped or considered a god.

Indians for centuries knew these water-dwellers but had been warned that one day the white man would live among the Indians and the water beings would not show themselves any more, although the Indians were assured that when this happened the Ojibway would still believe in them. The water beings lived away from the eyes of the white man, for it is said that they were afraid that he might expose them to public view, but the Ojibway never did want to find out who they really were; they met the water-dwellers as good friends. Indians for centuries used to offer gifts, as well as tobacco and firewater that were brought by the traders.

Once a water being told the Ojibway, "Never let a young woman see us, for it is taboo and we shall not appear again at the cliffs." This word was respected until one day a young woman covered by a buckskin blanket took a peek at them. The water beings never showed themselves again. Even to this day they are never seen, but it is believed that these beings are there yet at Nipigon Bay. No more offerings are made to them directly, but once in a while, if an Indian is caught in a storm, he offers tobacco and the waters become very calm. The present generation, however, does not practise the things done by their fathers.

It is said among the Ojibway that the water beings were very wise and powerful. They lived in all the waters of the lakes as we do on land. They were seen by the Ojibway from east to west and from south to north. They are men, women and children and they live on fish, but I cannot say here that they live forever as I believe they must die as we do. It is said that our ancestors traded tobacco and pipes with them in return for medicine that was very powerful. They spoke a little differently from us of the Ojibway, as their name was Maymaygwaysiwuk, that means in English "a person that speaks strangely."

These Maymaygwaysiwuk were also powerful dream guardians. If an Ojibway Indian, when fasting, dreamed of these beings he would become strong enough to prevent a sorcerer from bringing him into his magic shaking tent. The water beings would help that Indian overcome the sorcery, for they had the power of knowing all matters upon the earth and the water.

When seen, according to the Ojibway, they had with them a stone boat with stone paddles. Some say the canoe moved alone, by some power. Also some say that they used to steal fish from nets. At one time they were chased in order to know who they were. The Maymaygwaysiwuk would head for the shore line of cliffs, and the stone boat would go right into the opening as if through a door, which would be shut when the Ojibway got to the place. No door was to be seen. This was very strange indeed. At other times their boat would sink where they lived. When the Ojibway got there all they would see were bubbles, then they would know who they were.

My ancestor, my great-great-grandfather four generations ago, whose name was Little Grouse, had a medicine dream concerning an offering rock where the water demigod Misshipeshu, in the form of a huge cat, spoke to him and advised him to put on the rock a sacred sign made out of onaman, the Ojibway sacred sand. It was in the summer, and the water demigod helped my great-great-grandfather to put its sign on the walls of the cliffs. From then on, until thirty years ago, Indians of that area offered gifts to Misshipeshu.

26

In those days only the Ojibway Indians were at Lake Nipigon, there was no white man and everything was quiet. Maybe this is the main reason all water beings were seen so freely. But when the white men came and brought with them fish nets, motorboats, airplanes and railroads, these beings, the Ojibway believe, moved to a quieter place. Ojibway Indians of Lake Nipigon had an offering rock erected to this huge cat. Offerings of copper pails were thrown into the water and black dogs as well as white dogs, decorated in the very best, were offered alive to the water god for it to eat. In the time of the early traders, traps, guns and firewater, as well as great amounts of tobacco, were also put into the water. This was done once a year around June, in order not to offend the water god and to bring good luck to all those who believed in these offerings. Canoes formed a circle at the offering rock, as these rites took place on the water.

This huge cat is believed by the Ojibway to be white in colour, with horns, and very powerful. It is believed to live in the water but why a cat lives in the water, or where it lived, is not known. There is another big demigod of the same cat family who was considered very evil, but was a spirit. If anyone dreamed of this big water demigod at the time of fasting it was believed to bring misfortune, not to the dreamer but to his children. For this cat had to be pleased; it lived on human flesh or souls, but also accepted offerings of white pups about six months old to replace human souls. These offerings, however, were made very seldom, for this demigod was never demanding.

This big water god, or spirit, knew both good and evil. It all depended on what kind of nature an Indian had. If he were good then he would have the power to do good. If he were bad then he was given power to do bad. But the true water god, the white one in colour, always brought good luck to all who respected him.

The last offerings were made to the demigod

at Lake Nipigon about thirty years ago. Now the offering rock is bare, for the water god Misshipeshu moved away.

I was told by certain people who have studied what was written in books supposed to represent Ojibway lore that there were no female goddesses, only gods. I do not believe this because of a story about Misshipeshu that I was told while I was at Longlac by Mr. Abraham, a good Indian and a friend of mine.

He told me his grandfather was a powerful medicine-man. One day while he was trapping at Look-Into Lake in the Longlac area, where the Indians feared this water god lived, there was a big thunderstorm. For three days and nights lightning poured all around this lake. The lake itself was big with a smaller lake beside it. On his way Mr. Abraham's grandfather noticed both the lakes were all one piece of water. On the lake itself much foam was floating and one cliff near the water was pretty nearly levelled. As he went further he noticed two white things floating around, picked them up with his paddle and saw they were two small dead offspring of the water god. Then where did these come from if there were only male demigods?

Maymaygwaysiwuk offspring in a medicine dream look small, round and hairy and they prove that there was sex life among them, too. I do not believe their being demigods or goddesses gave them the power to create a young one through thought. Also I firmly believe that there were female goddesses. But according to Ojibway custom and beliefs the male is superior to all life and the female is set aside.

Also Misshipeshu, the watch god of the shaking tent ceremony, was a powerful demigod and had children by his female partner. Or perhaps if they were all only males he would say, "Now I am getting centuries old, it's about time for a new demigod, let there be one by my power."

Misshipeshu the Water God

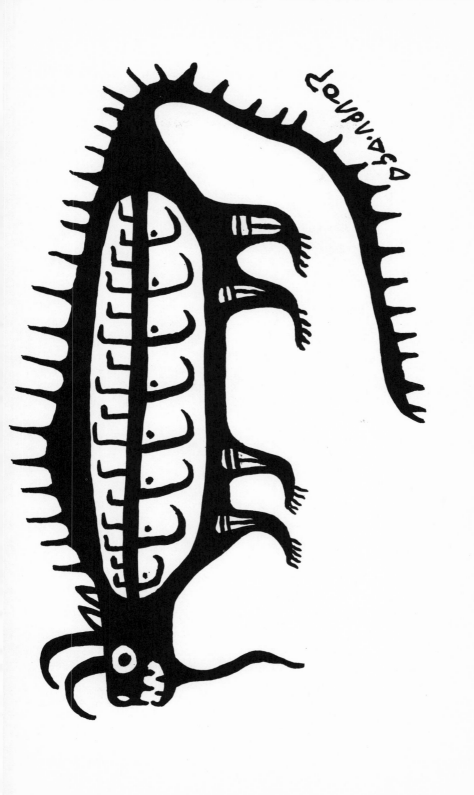

No, I do not think he had that power, no matter what power he had. After all, there was a power greater than he was, and the right to command offspring by thought was not his.

At one time Misshipeshu, the water demigod, lived at Lake Superior. One day late in the summer two Ojibway Indians, man and wife, with their little baby, came upon a big beach and both felt hungry. The Indian said to his wife, "I will go into the great forest to hunt some partridge, as they are plentiful, and you, my wife, gather some firewood. Leave our baby at the canoe side."

About half an hour later both returned to find their baby gone. By the shores of Lake Superior paw prints were seen and they were Misshipeshu's prints. The baby had been taken, cradle and all, into the water and into the underwater caves. What could the poor Indians do? Despite the loss of their child the Indian spoke, "I will play my medicine drum and ask the thunderbirds to destroy the cave, including Misshipeshu."

From the heavens appeared a great thunderbird that threw lightning into the caves and rocks. Misshipeshu was forced to come out. As the demigod was about to leave, the thunderbird struck the ground and Misshipeshu died from the lightning.

Meanwhile the couple fell into a coma, not knowing what really had taken place. When they awoke later they found their child's cradle floating on the surface of the water, their child dead with two holes in his head, and Misshipeshu's head floating around, the rest of his body having been eaten.

At Lake Superior another version of this legend was told to me by Luke Nanakonagos. An Indian family was travelling one summer near the area called Agawa Rock. On one of the beaches the Ojibway Indian said to his wife, "Let us make a fire, to eat." They left for the bush, the woman to get wood, the man for bark, leaving their only child, wrapped in a tikinagan, or carrier, near the

31

canoe, although the old-time Ojibway feared Lake Superior.

On returning they found their baby gone. When they looked at the sand, they saw Misshipeshu's footprints. The tracks were seen leading into the water, with the baby. The couple did not know what to do. Finally the man spoke, "I will call on my protectors, the birds of thunder, to come to our help. Although we shall not see our child again, I will do what I can through the help of my protectors. Let us now go under the canoe," and then he started to play his drum.

In about half an hour the thunderbirds, or thunderstorm, arrived in that area. The lightning began to pour on a mountain close by and it got dark. For two hours the storm lasted. Misshipeshu tried to hide but lightning fell all over the place and he was killed. Then the rain and lightning ceased, the skies cleared and the sun shone again. On the waters of Lake Superior, by the shore, an empty cradle was seen floating and beside it two small dead cubs. So ends this legend.

An old Ojibway Indian at Lake Nipigon had six sons and each summer one died of sickness. Finally the youngest of the sons, who was sixteen years old, was the only one left alive. One summer day the Ojibway Indian set out for the Orient Bay rock painting site and took with him a bundle of goods, including tobacco, and placed it on the waters and said, "Great Misshipeshu, hear my plea. I ask you by your power to save my only child. I offer these. In return, show me a sign that my plea is heard." The Indian went further down the bay, and when he reached Reflection Lake Camps on Lake Nipigon, behold, from the bottom of the water, he saw two eyes looking at him, which came to the surface with a splash. It was a very huge, red sturgeon, the keeper, or watcher, of the offering rock. This he believed was a sign of good luck, and from that day the only son recovered and lived.

It was claimed by the great Ojibway medicine-men that this large sturgeon was seen from time to time, also another really big sturgeon with a red belly and a box-shaped head. This the Ojibway believed to be a snake sturgeon and that whoever eats this evil snake sturgeon will become a snake or be smothered by them. This occurred twice, at Lake Nipigon and in the Longlac area.

It is not really known, as no written record was left, what really took place. But my own belief is that there must have been something in the sturgeon itself or its blood that attracted the snakes, which smothered the Indians after they were asleep. Perhaps the Indians became sick from eating this fish and could not help themselves after eating it, or else the meat turns into that poisonous matter after it is eaten.

The Ojibway of the Lake Nipigon area held Lake Hanna as a very sacred lake and called it Mesinama Sahegun. At each end of the lake were erected offering rocks to the evil snake sturgeons, and Indians travelling through this lake placed offerings of tobacco there so that no harm would come to them. The Ojibway did not travel in one part of this lake that was believed to be the place where these sturgeons lived, but the other side of the lake was fit for travel. But the Ojibway still left offerings of tobacco for them there, in order not to offend them.

The water of this lake was very dark in colour, not like Lake Nipigon water. Indians used to go to this lake to feast on the good sturgeons there. The Ojibway believed the snake sturgeon never existed here until one night it fell from the heavens with a mighty roar. Two years later these snake sturgeons with box-shaped heads were seen spawning among the good sturgeons. The Ojibway never feared these snake sturgeons and they did not know what effect one would have if eaten. About ten years later Ojibway Indians of that area ate this sturgeon and about two hundred families perished at their summer camp at Lake Hanna.

This story concerns the Ojibway Indians who were living at Nimpego Sahekun, Nipigon Lake. They used to move freely among the islands during the summer months, preparing for the long winter ahead. At the lake called Mesinama Sahegun, which is now under many feet of water due to the hydro dam at Pine Portage, the Ojibway Indians used to go to feast on the sturgeons. Everyone was happy. The old women and the young prepared smoked sturgeon and put it away in birchbark containers for the long winter months ahead.

It was the custom of the Ojibway to take a girl who was about to become a woman into the woods until she was safe to go among the young men, since she was taboo. Nekahnee Bahnasik, Leader of Bird Women, was one of these girls and about fifteen years of age at the time. Her nokomis, that is, her grandmother, took her into the woods and advised her thus, "My granddaughter, I have made a place for you as it is the custom of our people and we must respect the Ojibway customs. I will leave you here until I come to get you again. Now I shall go into the village to prepare nama, the sturgeon, for the great feast, as we have invited many to attend. I am leaving enough deer meat and fish to last you until tomorrow."

Meantime at the summer village at Lake Hanna everyone was preparing for the feast. Two days passed and still her nokomis had not returned for Nekahnee Bahnasik. The girl wondered at this and thought to herself, "Why has not my grandmother come to see me and brought me something to eat?" She had an uneasy feeling and sensed that something might be wrong. So she decided to visit the village, taboo or not.

Nekahnee Bahnasik covered the mile back to her village very quickly. As she approached she noticed the lack of smoke from the wigwams, no voices of children playing, and not even the bark of a dog to greet her. The poor girl was not prepared for the sight that awaited her. The wigwam of her nokomis was the first in the village. As she

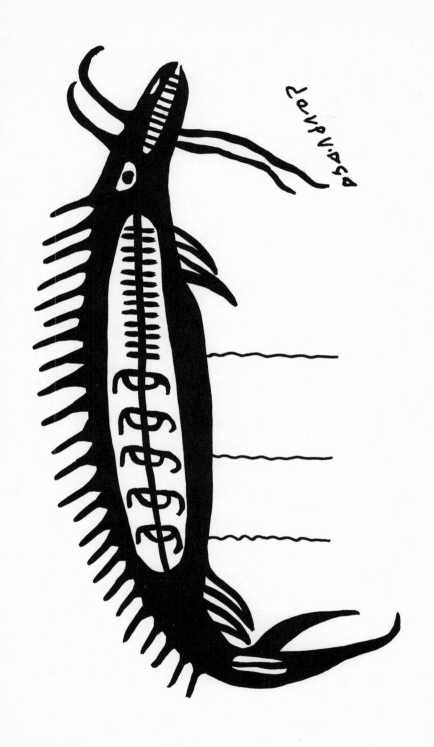

opened the flap she was horrified to see snakes of every size writhing on the ground. She ran in panic and fear to open the flaps of other wigwams. She found nothing but snakes. On the poles where the sturgeon meat had been hung to dry, in the cooking pots, in the bark containers, all that was left was the good-eating kind of sturgeon. Her people as they retired must have turned into snakes.

As she approached the last wigwam she thought to herself, "Surely, someone must have survived." How thankful she was when she noticed a cradle in which was lying a small papoose. She grabbed the cradle and took the child with her.

She was now grateful to the Great Manitou, the one God, because she had come of age. Had she been at the feast she would no doubt have perished, too. Her people must have eaten this strange-looking sturgeon. Possibly someone had said, "Let us eat this sturgeon. Perhaps it is as good as the other kind." This terrible mistake of the Ojibway was to be a lesson to future generations.

What was Nekahnee Bahnasik to do? She quickly made up her mind to take the baby and some necessities and set out for Lake Nipigon. After many portages she arrived at Kinook Gumming (Longlac), and told her sad story. "My people noticed these sturgeons spawning among the other good sturgeons. They were black, with dark red bellies. Some were ten to fifteen feet in length with box-shaped heads."

There was no disbelief or doubt as she explained what had happened to her people. An old chief told her, "This is indeed the devilfish snake fish. Whoever eats this fish will become a snake. What causes this I do not know and cannot explain. Something of this nature happened to six families of Ojibway Indians at Devilfish Lake."

This type of sturgeon was seen until fifty years ago. The Indians of this area do not know what kind of fish it was, nor do our white brothers.

I often wonder if these things really happened. Our white brothers experiment to find out things. Let us see if they could set big nets and trap a snake sturgeon for the public to see. Lake Hanna is dammed under water, but Manito Namiege is still as it was, and if this story is true the sturgeons must still be there.

THE
SACRED BEAR BELIEFS
OF
THE MIDAYWEWIN

The Midaywewin Society of the Ojibway held this animal to be sacred. Legend states that the bear was at one time in the early history of the Ojibway a human, or had human form. Then it turned into an animal. It is indeed strange to say that a bear understands Indian, but if Indians meet a bear, in fear they address it as "Our grandfather to all of us, the Ojibway," and start to talk to it. It is a great sight to see a bear's ears and head moving as you speak to it. Those Indians whom the bear wanted to fight had been told the bear would release its hold and stop being angry if addressed properly. Its meat has to be smoked, as it cannot be eaten fresh for fear of diarrhoea, or shits. To the Indian way of thinking, a person gets shits not through the meat itself but because the bear is sacred, and one cannot eat too much of the meat of a demigod.

So powerful is the sacred bear that all the bear's bones were used for charms and relics for sucking rites. One sees a whole string full of bear's bones from all parts of the body in two-inch lengths. During these rites the medicine man starts to suck and rattle with these bones. A hollow bone from a leg or arm cut to a certain size is used for sucking out disease or sickness brought on by sorcery. Claws are kept, also. Teeth, especially the two front teeth, are made into whistles as charms. For a bear is so powerful over other animals and demigods that to blow its tooth puts fear into the spirits. Fur, meat and oil are used, and poisons as well as medicine are made from the gall. Clothing and tobacco are tied with one claw in bright-coloured cloth and ribbon and placed in the forest in its honour. The bear's shoulders are painted and used as a charm for long life. Say an Indian is fifty years old today, he would take a shoulder-blade and would then start putting marks on it, say five. Each mark told how many years he wished to live. When that time was up more marks were added, and so forth.

According to Ojibway custom, bear skulls are sacred. I have four in my home, carefully decorated and painted with oils in red, blue, yellow and white that really make these charms colourful. The Indians used to paint in those colours when they could be obtained. Before paint, red matter or earth colours replaced the paint we use today. According to a medicine dream, the sacred bear is white in colour, has red feet with yellow spots, and two horns. To possess the white skin of an albino bear meant honour to the Ojibway. The owner would be respected by all and the fur divided up for charm pipes and bags or kept just as a whole skin. In the same way the Plains Indians held sacred the albino buffalo.

Ojibway Indians of Lake Nipigon had what is known as the Midaywewin Society. An Ojibway, or his family, had to pay a great quantity of goods to be a member of this society. In addition, the new member would have to pass some test. At the Midaywewin Lodge would be a great table and on the table would be all kinds of good food to eat. On another table would be pots full of partly cooked dog meat and broth. In order to pass the test a person would be required to eat great amounts of dog soup and meat. Also live snakes were brought into the ceremony and their tails cut off and swallowed down while still wriggling. Some Indians who were full members were known to have swallowed six tails, but a lot of people started to throw up. Certain food that was con-

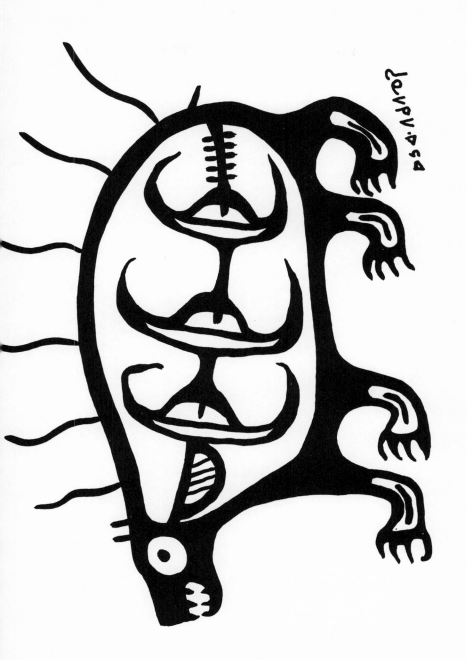

sidered bad medicine was also placed on the table. Some full-fledged members were known to eat these bad medicine dishes with no ill effects. These were the tests. If a person could not pass them it was hard to be a member.

Each member had some kind of hide such as otter, weasel, bear, marten, fisher, mink or fox. During the Midaywewin ceremonies these hides were seen to come alive. The bearskin began to growl and the fox skins began to bark, for these were the medicine hides of the members. The new member would do his best to join the society and a medicine bag was given to him to help him in these tests. He would be asked to point this bag at another new member. Out of the medicine bag would shoot forth medicine, or magic powers. The Indian would fall to the ground, spitting blood and dying from the effects of the powerful medicine bag, but would be revived again as if nothing had happened.

At Gull Bay, Ontario, long ago, the early Ojibway who made a settlement used to hold what is called the White Dog Feast. Two white dogs were fattened up and were brought to the Midaywewin Lodge, killed, and had all their hair burned off. After being cleaned and scraped they were cut up and put into huge pots. A big circle would be made, with a fish net put around it for decoration. Inside the circle a long row of bark would be placed. Then the elders of Midaywewin knowledge would be seated and one appointed Indian would take from the pot some partly cooked white dog. The two dog heads, with the blood still dripping red, were offered to the two Midaywewin elders, who said before eating, "Let everyone who eats this dog say that they are eating a bear, for this is bear itself, not a dog." Then the elders began to eat in a manner that would make anyone turn his head in the other direction; there was blood in their mouths and on their hands. After this large bowls of dog soup were offered. They ate just as we would eat a T-bone steak and black coffee. But, as I said, there were no side effects. I understand the elders took medicine in order not to be affected.

Later each member would bring out Midaywewin bags of powerful medicine, each with its otter skin. An Ojibway woman would then take up the big bearskin that was tied to some poles and her husband, through his power, commanded the skin to come alive and it would crawl and try to get itself loose from the buckskin strings that tied it. All the otter skins that were running around would jump into the medicine bags in fear of the bear.

There were half-breeds there who had no faith in the ceremony. One happened to be a pugilist boxer, a big-set fellow who knew his trade. A Midaywewin member got up to add a new member to the society. The half-breeds looked in amazement at what was about to take place. The Midaywewin member brought out a bag and opened it before a new member. The power of great medicine shot forth from the bag. The new member fell back on the ground, blood running out of his nose and mouth, in a death-like trance. Then another new member was given another bag and revived him. This was the test he had to pass.

The half-breed who was a pugilist boxer spoke to the full-fledged Midaywewin member and said, "I could do the same, only it takes time to revive a fallen person."

Then the Midaywewin member said, "Show me your power. Who gave you this power, when you do not believe in anything?"

That was it. Bang went the half-breed's fist across the mouth of the Midaywewin member and coolly knocked him out. His movements were too fast to follow. He asked for water. Down it went upon the Midaywewin member. Slowly he revived.

The Ojibway being good-natured, everyone began to laugh, including the Midaywewin member, who slowly said, "Although a half-breed, your power is greater than ours, nevertheless for our

44

ancestors' sake let us continue to use the power we were taught by them."

The Thunderbird Midaywewin Society was the Lake Superior branch of the Midaywewin Society. All these societies study all kinds of medicine.

My grandfather on my father's side at the time of his fasting year had a great medicine dream of a bear. The bear said to him in his medicine dream, "My son, I will be a guardian to you and give you some special power. Although you will not be a conjurer or a medicine-man, still you shall have power to do good. I will also give you good luck, but you must respect me in my earthly form and never kill me. Now I will go into your body." According to that medicine dream my grandfather believed that there was a bear inside his body. He felt its presence at his back, or hip.

One day he met some Ojibway Indians who were known to be great conjurers. They drank some firewater — whisky — and got drunk. Some hours later a fight started among them as to who was powerful in the Ojibway magic arts. My grandfather said to the conjurers, "I am not good at conjuring and I will not boast, but I am good with my fists," and gave the conjurers a good licking. Then one of the conjurers said to my grandfather, "Some day I will get the better of you yet," and this he did in the matter of a year.

Through the bad medicine of evil conjuring, the bear inside my grandfather was poisoned and my grandfather fell sick about one week later. A medicine-man who was my grandfather's relation was called from Fort Frances and tried his best to cure him, but it was too late. The medicine-man had all kinds of bones of animals and bears, for he was a member of the Midaywewin Society. He rubbed and also sucked with a big Ojibway medicine sucking bone about twelve inches long, but was unable to cure my grandfather.

He did what was to be done, however, and sucked out the affected part at the back. As he did this he said aloud, "Now I will show you what was done to you." In his hand the medicine-man had a small bear about four inches long, with a piece of chewing-tobacco and strands of human hair in its mouth. My grandfather did not like the sight or smell of chewing-tobacco or human hair. He did not like to find hair in the food that was cooked for him, when hair sometimes fell into the cooking. This was how the bear was conjured.

After this my grandfather (my father's father, not Moses, my mother's father) did not feel right but managed to live for a while and died about one year later.

GREAT MEDICINES
OF THE
OJIBWAY PEOPLE

Medicine in the Ojibway tribe was very important, and the Indians knew over three hundred kinds that they got from the water as well as the land. The emblem for medicine in the Ojibway tribe was a horned snake. A man who dreamed of a horned snake, or serpent, was considered to be a medicine-man and to have knowledge of medicine, and even if he did not become a medicine-man at least he would have true knowledge of medicine.

We in the Ojibway tribe have medicine-men and women. Some medicine-men were very great in their skill or trade and did not need to gather or prepare medicine. All they would do was to have an empty birchbark dish covered with a clean deer hide or cloth. When the medicine-man was called to attend a sick person he would play his sacred medicine drum and place the dish outside. After he had played his medicine song the dish would be brought inside and in it would be very small bundles of sacred medicine that are believed by the Ojibway to be placed there by the medicine serpent.

Other Ojibway medicines were based on the thunderbirds. This society of Ojibway medicine was called the Thunderbird Medicine Society. It is an Ojibway belief that the great thunderbird in a medicine dream gives power to the dreamer to prepare medicine. Also it is believed that, for those who learn from the thunderbirds, medicines are not made out of roots, barks and so on but are in the form of an egg of a light-blue colour. Other medicine matter was red, yellow or white. When a thunderbird medicine-man prepared medicine he

47

would scrape the egg and some of the powder would be placed in a small pail. Sometimes small medicine eggs were dropped whole in the medicine pots. These were used for curing the sick.

The Indians used a sickness called the crooked-mouth sickness to harm their fellow Indians. This sickness is brought on by the conjurer if an Indian should offend one of his fellows. The offended party would go to the conjurer who could perform this rite and ask for the culprit to be given a crooked mouth. I understand that the medicine-man was given the power by tying a frog on a cross, sewing up its mouth and pulling it sideways. While doing this he would go into a spell and ask the evil spirits to assist him and, sure enough, the Indian who had said bad things would get a crooked mouth. Other means are also used, for each medicine-man has his own way of doing evil. If some of this bad medicine were put into your drink you would have a crooked mouth. Some Indians die from this as they cannot eat. But let us not give up hope. I will explain how the patient finds a cure, for there is a cure, as well as medicine to treat this illness.

If an Indian should get this sickness, first he would have a sore eye and think it was some eye disease. Then he would feel his skin being drawn down to one side, little by little, until in a week's time his mouth would begin to drop until it was crooked. There is no pain at any time.

There is one Indian still alive today who had this sickness, for I saw it myself. After one week he went to a doctor to be cured, but was advised by the doctor that there was nothing wrong with him and that he might have had a stroke, or perhaps had been sweating and got cold. The Indian, however, knew what was wrong, went to a medicine-man and was cured. Today you will not notice any trace of his sickness except very slightly around his mouth. Many Indians had this sickness a long time ago, but very few today.

48

The Indians had to find a cure for this illness, and the cure was given to them by the good spirits and by the spirits of the dead.' When an Ojibway Indian is fasting in his fasting years he will dream of a certain dead person, who will advise him to take a piece of his bone to cure people of the crooked-mouth sickness, saying, "I will give you power to make this bone of mine into medicine." The bone is a piece taken from the left side of a human head and then treated with all the magic rites of the Ojibway. This is called the Ojibway relic-bone medicine. Two long needles are used, which are scraped against the bone, and a medicine spark comes from it as if it were flint. The needles are jabbed lightly against the lower part of the ear or top part of the cheek bones of the sick person and after a few treatments the patient gets better and his mouth returns to normal. This treatment is used in cases where the conjurer who caused the sickness had asked the bad spirits to assist him.

Sometimes herbs and bad medicine are used for a person who has this sickness. These are often given the patient to drink, or are put in a place—perhaps a spring—where he would drink. But no spirits are asked to assist, only bad medicine is used. There is also a cure for this. Good medicine is used instead of relic medicine.

To make an Indian go crazy the conjurer ties a snake by the tail. Then the Indian goes crazy in the same way as the snake does trying to unloose itself.

Some Indians claim otter liver will cure fits in children. Beaver castors are used as medicine. All the herbs in the forest are used by the Ojibway, as well as tree roots and barks. Small tobacco offerings were placed where a herb had been removed by some Indians who belonged to the medicine societies, although not many followed this custom. Mostly they would wait until all the medicine was gathered, then play their medicine drums and smoke the sacred pipes in honour of the spirits for all the medicine gathered.

There is one root, or water herb, that grows on the waters, which has long green leaves and at the bottom its roots are solidly based and tubular in shape. These roots are good for colds and are powerful medicine against snakes. Indians would grind these roots to fine powders and place the powder around their dwellings.

There was a lady at Nipigon, Ontario, who was known for her skill as a midwife and was also experienced in helping women during pregnancy. This Indian lady had a medicine she gave her patients and they felt no pain, or very little, when having babies. I was told that she was trapping on one of the Lake Superior islands with her husband when she saw that a moose on that island had two calves that spring, and she noticed where the moose had chewed off some bark at that time. When she asked her husband why a moose would do this he told her that the moose did it in order not to feel pain and that it was nature's way of helping animals. An idea came to her to try this out on a human patient who was about to give birth, and it proved to be very successful with no side effects whatsoever.

The Ojibway had what we call a steam house that looked like an upside-down bowl, made out of saplings and covered with hide or canvas, with a floor cover of cedar branches. Indians of the Ojibway tribe used this steam house to cure certain sicknesses that bothered them. Red-hot stones are placed inside and water is poured upon them to give steam. All kinds of sweet-smelling herbs are burned, but among the Ojibway tribe of Lake Nipigon dried cedar is mostly used. At the same time it cleans a man's body and his soul. It was believed that after an Indian purified himself the spirits came more easily in medicine dreams and he had a better chance to speak to the Great Spirit. The steam bath was used by certain medicine-men to talk to the water god, thunderbird or medicine snakes, as well as to ask nature to give better weather.

An Ojibway Indian going inside a steam house would take a small stick and place sweet-smelling herbs on the rock or stones and pour water on them and say, "Oh, stones, for centuries you have been hot and dry, now I place water upon you. Help me to speak better to my God and the spirits," and he would then start pounding on the rocks and chanting Indian sacred songs. These lasted for many hours.

The Ojibway of Lake Nipigon had two kinds of steam bathhouses. One was made to be used for cures, and spirits would be asked to assist through the steam house. And there was one steam bath that was erected to the thunderbird. This was made on a platform and stood about two or three feet above the ground. Ojibway Indians made these for their own use, as well as for the medicine-man. The one that stood on the ground was not valued very much but the one that stood above the ground was considered very valuable, and if an Indian made this for an elder or medicine-man, in return he would get rich rewards from them.

Some of the red onaman sand was used for love medicine and another sand that was coloured light red was mixed with grease and used for a medicine rub for rubbing on the affected parts of the body. These sands were never drunk. The Ojibway also had a bluish-coloured onaman sand that was used as a sacred charm against conjuring. There was, too, a white-coloured sand that cured headaches when a small amount was placed on a heated stone, also a white liquid to cure pains. All these can still be obtained in the Lake Nipigon area, although none are used at this time.

Among the Ojibway medicine-men of Lake Nipigon I have seen the use of the sacred onaman sand that the Ojibway pick up from the earth. To give an example to the reader, not long ago, in the year 1962, I was in the dwelling of my aged grandfather, Potan, when one night a stranger came all the day down from Pembroke, Ontario, to see my grandmother who had died, not my real grandmother, that is, but a close cousin to my grandfather whom custom required that I should address as grandmother.

This visitor, a woman, told my grandfather that she was sorry to know my grandmother was dead, for she was indeed a great medicine-woman. The visitor said, "I am sick in my right arm and hand. I cannot move them, due to sorcery in this modern age. The sickness started because two men began to fight and I took away the gun of one of them whose mother was a sorceress. She told me she would take her revenge and that this would happen." She had sought medical aid from the white man's doctors and was advised that there was not much to be done, but she knew that medicine rites among the Indians were more powerful. After all, what white doctor could say that he could cure sorcery? To modern thinking, it is all of the mind.

My grandfather told this woman, "If I were in the same position as you I would kill this sorceress by sorcery, in revenge. But although I cannot interfere in this matter, if you seek my aid I will cure you."

My grandfather told me to assist him in the sacred rites and medicine songs. From his bag he took a bottle of onaman, the light earth-coloured sand of my people, and he was going to use lard to put on her arms. I said to my grandfather, "That is a mistake, instead of lard let us use bear grease." The bear grease is rubbed all over the patient's arms, the medicine sands are sprinkled over the grease and one begins to rub toward the fingers. One starts from the top joint of the arm, rubbing toward the fingers as if the medicine-man were pushing the sickness out of the patient. These primitive rites are hard for modern people to believe. But if one witnesses these rites one has to believe, especially if a patient's arm was numb

54

and swollen and the fingers useless, and then after one week he regains all his movements as if no sickness had ever been there. In this manner my grandfather cured the woman.

Centuries ago, when the Midaywewin sacred bear appeared to the early Ojibway and gave them the sacred knowledge of several hundred kinds of medicine through a horned serpent, the medicines were represented by a cup. The demigod said to the Ojibway, "This cup I give you shall never overflow. It must always be kept at a certain level. In order to keep it at this level, from henceforth all generations shall seek knowledge through fasting." Very few have tried to keep it at that level, and the cup has now reached the stage where it will overflow because the younger people are not interested in keeping that medicine culture alive.

A sign was shown to the Ojibway long ago, and today the demigod of medicine through the horned serpent still gives this knowledge to some, even without fasting. Can that cup be kept the same as before or will it overflow and be destroyed? If destroyed, the great medicine culture of my Ojibway ancestors will die with them. I wish as I am writing that you, my people, would try to preserve our precious knowledge by encouraging our younger people to take an interest in it.

LOVE CHARMS, SEXUAL LORE AND LEGENDS

All young people of the Ojibway tribe were married at an early age to preserve the race, and to prevent any children on the side. No Indian was ever a homosexual or sex-crazed person. There were no rapes or any of the other sexual crimes that we find among people today. There were no bachelors or old maids; some chiefs had extra wives, although only a few followed this custom.

The Ojibway Indians of the Lake Nipigon area would go to a frog pond in early spring, and if a man saw two mating frogs he would make a sharp-pointed stick and try to pierce them together without separating them and would say, "In the same manner that you are enjoying together, let me be loved by the woman that I desire to be loved by." The two frogs would be dried in that position, and when the Indian tired of his partner he would hit the frogs apart and the love-spell would release its hold on her.

Onaman sand, the light-coloured Indian medicine found in the earth, is gathered by the Ojibway and the sorcerer blesses it with Ojibway rites, mixes with it bits of the hair of the desired person and a dried frog ground with a sparrow's head, and ties it all together in a small hide bag. This is worn as a charm for love.

Ojibway would rub bear oil that had been treated with special rites upon their private parts in order to have a good sexual life.

The Indians were often easily offended. Everyone carried medicine, and if a man were offended he would fix his enemy through evil charms and conjuring. As this story goes, there was an old man at Fort Frances long ago who had a daughter and another old man who had a son. One day the son went to the other Ojibway Indian to ask for his daughter and was told to take her but he was unable to do so until the next spring, for this was in the fall of the year. The young man told his future bride that he had to make a place for them to stay but that he would be back in the spring, and he left his bride.

The woman's father was very offended at this and said, "Why did he not take my daughter now? I will fix him up." About half-way up to the winter camp at one of the portages the young warrior felt as if someone had shot him in the leg and he could not move it.

The father of the young warrior was a bad medicine-man. Also he loved his son and he knew that he was being conjured by means of a shotgun. He told him to lie down and started to suck the leg and afterwards spat on it. Blood and lead shotgun pellets appeared on the ground, and in this manner he cured his son.

Now the old man spoke: "I will fix that woman's dad for doing this." Out of his underclothing he brought a little bag containing deadly poison, dipped a small feather in it, blew upon the feather and said, "Go with the help of my guardian spirits. Go to the one that tried to kill my son through conjuring." And that was that.

Next spring the young man came and got his maid but he did not notice her father around. He asked his woman, "Where is your father?"

"Oh," replied the lady, "my father died very suddenly after you left and I do not know what happened to him, except that I know he was poisoned."

This is the Fort Alexander conjurer story. There was a young man who was very handsome, and a certain woman asked his parents to arrange a marriage according to the custom of the Saulteaux

57

tribes, a branch of Indians closely related to the Ojibway. The young Indian refused and said, "I don't want you for a wife for you do not match my looks." This being an insult to the Indian woman, she went to her father, a sorcerer, to seek revenge. That night the woman cut the hair from her private parts and tied it to a small piece of chewing tobacco, and this was handed to her father, who enclosed it in a special drum and went into a trance. When the drum was opened there was nothing in it.

Meantime the package was already on its way to be implanted into the man's right leg, close to his private parts. About ten days later he complained of soreness and could not move. Every herb was tried without success. Finally a man who was skilled in sorcery was called to perform his curing rites. It was night and the medicine-man was seated close to his patient, with onlookers there. The medicine-man looked into his bag and placed two bones about one inch long on a clean birchbark cup to be used in the sucking rites.

He started to play his drum and as he played he said to the bones, "Come forward, O bones of the sacred bear." Each bone lifted into the air and flew gently into the patient's mouth. Then the medicine-man said to the onlookers, "Turn out the lights of the lamps," and as he bent down to start his rites stars were seen twinkling on his back, showing that power was in him. When the lights were turned on he spat out on to a dish of bark a package of tobacco and hair from a woman's private parts, and the young man was cured. Then they knew who had caused this. They took their revenge and she died unwanted.

There is a legend concerning giants, or big people, who lived before the Flood. According to Ojibway mythology, at that far-away time an Indian was travelling with his canoe across a big lake. Upon reaching shore he noticed huge footprints on the sands. Being scared and knowing

they were made by the big people, he fled into the forest to hide. As the giants were approaching the direction where he was hiding, one of them, seeing his small footprints, said to another, "Look on the sands, brother. Do you see the prints of a baby? Let us look for him." When the Indian was found he was hiding behind a stump. Then the big people took the Indian to their father, to whom they presented him, saying, "Father, we have brought you a baby. Let us put him in a cradle."

Then the father giant spoke to his sons: "I want you to take this 'baby' back where you got him. Don't you know that he is an Indian, one of the rulers of the earth? We should respect him like a demigod."

But for some reason the brothers did not take the Indian back. Later that night the youngest daughter of the big people took him home and exiled herself to a far land. (In addition, I was also told that the youngest sister of the big people married the Indian. That will have to be studied.)

The Ojibway call a woman's monthly period "my grandmother." One day I came home from work and my wife told me I had had a visitor that morning, and she said her grandmother was there. I did not know what she meant until I started to think, then I realized.

One time a very old Ojibway Indian named Red Sky said to another Ojibway, "I remember the time I was in my mother's womb. The heart of my mother was thunder. When my mother passed water it was my river. I felt as if I lived inside a wigwam. I had my door and the belly for a window. I was a woman at the time, but because my feet were crooked and that would spoil my appearance if I were a woman the Great Spirit spoke to me through my mother and said, 'Red Sky, I will let you be a man instead of a woman.'"

There lived among the Ojibway a very jealous woman who was extremely jealous of her husband, although he never did anything to make her so.

61

But this was her nature. We say everything has its beginning, or reasons. Finally the old chief, who was also a medicine-man known to have cured people, curing the mind by unloading its troubles, asked this woman, "Let me and some of our elders help you. Tell us the reason you are this way. I am sure we could help you."

The woman said, "I know you could help me. I have faith in you but I am too shy to tell you what I have to say. May I write it down in Cree syllabics?"

The chief said, "If you feel you should, unburden yourself on paper and we will help you."

A few days later she gave the chief a letter stating what she thought was the cause of her jealousy. This is what the letter said, as told to me orally.

"When I was fifteen years old I went into the forest to fast for two days. I neither ate nor drank. The last night I dreamed of a big river. On the river was floating a huge bag. Thinking in my dream it was a medicine bag, I waited by the riverside that was covered with smooth rocks. The bag came in my direction. I picked it up and opened it. The first thing that I got out was a man's private parts, his nuts, then another, until I had emptied the bag. I placed the nuts on the rocks. They were of all sizes, small, medium and large. I was then told to pick up and sort out the ones I wanted to keep and place the others back in the bag. I took all the nice ones I liked and tried them and I threw the rest back in the river in the bag.

"I awoke and came home. From then on I wished I had tried them all but I cannot. That is why I turn against my husband in jealousy."

They all laughed. In accordance with the rites of the cure, she got better and became a good wife. So ends this story.

There is an Ojibway story about a pretty girl called Mowiss. Many men fell in love with her but she only played the field and never had any intention whatever of falling in love.

62

There was one young Ojibway who fell deeply in love with her and after he fell in love with her she dropped him. This made him very angry. He said to himself, "If I am not the one to love her then she shall never love another. She took me for a fool but I will fix her."

First, he went straight to the human manure pile and gathered enough to mould a figure of a man. In the meantime he had ordered all the necessary clothing required for the figure. He then gathered white dog dung and rubbed this on its face to make the complexion brighter. After this he placed the figure in a birchbark canoe. This occurred during the early or late spring.

In the lady's village the people saw a stranger waving from across the river. They went to meet him to accompany him back to their camp. They asked him where he came from and where he was bound. He said, "I am just passing through." So they asked him if he were hungry or thirsty but he said, "No, I take refreshment only if it is luke-warm." They asked him if he were cold and invited him to sit by their fire. Again he refused, saying, "I am afraid of evaporating." He stood many feet away from the fire to escape any heat.

When the lady heard of this stranger she went to see him and fell head over heels in love with him, not realizing that he was meant for her all along. She asked him when he was leaving and he replied, "Tomorrow." She was very unhappy because she was in love with him and she had never felt like that toward any man before.

The stranger left the following morning, three hours before the lady found that he was gone. So she followed him. A few miles down the trail she noticed a mitt, further on another mitt, and so on till she had found all his clothing. Finally the trail ended. All she found was a pile of dung. She was embarrassed and ashamed and felt a fool because of all she had been through. So this is how the story ends.

ALLERGIES AND DREAMS
OF THE OJIBWAY
OF THE
NIPIGON AREA

A lot of Indians are allergic to various things, such as sturgeon, rabbit, moose and deer.

There is living today an Ojibway Indian of Lake Nipigon whom we shall call Jogoway, as he is allergic to moose meat. At one time he loved this meat. Then he dreamed he killed a moose. Upon coming close to it he felt funny. He proceeded to clean the meat. Then Jogoway knew it was a human being he cleaned and the meat he had eaten was human.

From that day on, little by little, Jogoway became allergic to moose. It is over twenty years since he ate moose and to this day he cannot eat it at all. Even if he smells moose meat frying he gets headaches and goes almost crazy.

Also a lady at Macdiarmid, Ontario, called Elizabeth, used to eat moose meat until one day she had a bad medicine dream and became allergic to it. One year later she became allergic also to beef, buttermilk and any part of a cow. She was even allergic to all kinds of pork and could not eat sausages or lard, bacon or salt pork. But she lived to a ripe old age, eating fish, potatoes, deer meat and other wild animals such as rabbit and wildfowl.

Nikeeg, an Ojibway Indian of Lake Nipigon in years gone by, never ate a lake trout, which were plentiful in the Lake Nipigon waters before the white man came to that area. This fish was a staff of life among the Ojibway living there. The Indians of this area would save all the rabbit leg bones and place bait on them in a fashion that was known among the Ojibway, in order to catch lake trout through the ice in the winter. This method was also used in summer, when the Ojibway had other means of catching lake trout. If the fish swallowed the baited bone whole, the bone got stuck sideways. The Ojibway of Lake Nipigon dried and smoked these fish, which were stored in big birchbark containers for winter use. Some were dried and pounded to powder and in that form were eaten with all kinds of berries.

Nikeeg who, as I said, did not eat lake trout was once asked why. "One day," said Nikeeg, "in a medicine dream I dreamed I was paddling my birchbark canoe in a big lake. At the other side of the lake I noticed a big cave, or tunnel, for it was dark. And I dreamed I paddled into this cave. When I looked I noticed teeth and I knew I had paddled into a lake trout and that I was inside the trout's belly. When I woke up I was afraid because I dreamed I did not come out. At one time I used to like eating trout for I was raised on this fish, but when I tried to eat it after this bad medicine dream I was unable to because I was now allergic to lake trout."

In days gone by, when the Ojibway still lived alone in this great country of ours, in the Lake Nipigon area it was a common thing for the young people to fast for a period of days. This was done so that the Indian lad or girl might know his guardian spirits. Many years ago, when I was only a boy, I dreamed of a great, huge lake. Toward the east came a great river. In this river of the eastern lake it was rough. It was not easy to get to this lake, which I will call the Great Medicine Lake of the East. At each portage lived serpents, the water demigod Misshipeshu and other creatures of the Ojibway belief. I was not at all afraid for I was in the company of the thunderbirds. When I got safely to the top of this lake I was told by my guardians that they would leave me there to find out for myself the things I should know in order to live a good life on earth.

I noticed across the lake three caves of life. Each cave had a medicine boat made out of onaman sand in the sacred colours of red, blue and white. I was told to choose my boat, or canoe, to take me to the medicine caves. I took the white one. I knew later that I had made the right choice. I stepped into the canoe and I was taken by some power into the caves. There I was shown the great Ojibway arts in conjuring, medicine charms, medicine pipes and bad and good medicine. I was shown sacred pipes of luck, stone medicines, sacred drums and songs and told to take whatever I needed. I did not pick up the things I saw except for life itself, which was in the form of a white feather.

How thankful I am to have made such a good choice.

I was taken out of these caves and in the middle of the lake stood a great moose, so big that the clouds bumped against his chest. It was the most wonderful sign I ever saw, even in a dream. There, on the side of the moose, were small Indians who shot arrows at it but were unable to harm it, as if the arrows were no more than tiny toothpicks. And when the great medicine moose stamped right or left with one of his legs it shook that part of the world.

My companions, the thunderbirds, returned to lead me out of this eastern lake. One of the birds spoke to me. "Do you see the great moose?"

I said, "Yes."

"You made the right choice when you picked life inside those medicine caves. That moose you saw is also life for it is strong, great, powerful and healthy. It is yourself. Some parts of the moose will be in you, to keep you and guard you all your life. Did you see the small Indians with arrows that looked like toothpicks? In those arrows are sicknesses of all kinds but they cannot affect the moose. Do not be afraid in life. You will be big, strong and healthy and the great moose shall keep you forever."

Then I awoke from my medicine dream, which I believe, for some of the things came true. I am big and healthy and strong, thanks to my medicine dream of the great moose that reached the very clouds.

Ojibway Indians never fasted when the leaves were all out. Legend states what befell one Ojibway Indian who did. One summer the leaves were out pretty near their full growth. The leaves looked at the Indian and each said, "I pity you, for I am green. I will give you life. I will be your guardian."

The Ojibway said, "Yes," not knowing the mistake he made.

That fall the Ojibway lad died, because the leaves live only one season and this Indian lived only one season also. That is why we are told never to fast at this time, but in early spring before the leaves are out there is a better chance not to repeat the same mistake.

One never fasted when the snow was on the ground either, lest Windigo, the most feared of evil demigods, should take a man's body as an instrument for his evil ways and make the Indian feel the longing to devour human flesh.

To dream of flying like a bird, without wings, foretells a long life. Also if a rabbit bites you in a dream or in reality this, too, foretells a long life.

To see clearly the face of a stranger or of family or friends in a dream foretells that you will see them or have a visit.

To dream of a new moon with a star beside it foretells that a stranger will visit your home.

A bear foretells good luck, and to dream of an eagle means honour, importance and the respect of friends.

A powerful dream is Manitou's protection against demigods and foretells that you will overcome sorcery and that Manitou will restore your peace of mind.

I am writing this dream of myself because it is important to give the reader an idea of how the Indian mind works when it is afraid. Although I am an Ojibway Indian artist and I paint the ancient art forms of the Ojibway, no Indian would ever take the step I took, for fear of the supernatural I have in a way broken a barrier, a taboo. I have no fear of anything but at same time I have a great respect for my ancestral beliefs.

Of course, being an Indian I had some fears at first, as if one jumps in a big lake only to land in two inches of water. In a way the supernatural is the same. One does not know what one goes into. The depth was unknown to me but I went right ahead and jumped in. If an Indian is afraid of the unknown it prevents him doing what he should do or should not do. But once he knows there is nothing there, as there was nothing to start with, then he goes ahead without fear. Before taking up my art to paint legends and art forms I had my doubts.

One night I had a great dream concerning direct protection from the Great Manitou, God of the ancient Ojibway, whom I believe to be the same as the Christian Godhead, God the Father of all human races. I believe this was a dream of great significance, inspired in me by Manitou himself.

I was in a place with the demigods whom I represent in art form. I saw two Misshipeshu and serpents of evil. I was not afraid for I felt a shadow protecting me. The demigods were devouring some matter. The shadow left me for I saw it moving behind me. I noticed the two huge paws of a great bear getting hold of me. Then I was afraid.

I got away from its hold and the place of the evil demigods, and I ran toward the shadow that had protected me as if I were running in a big clearing. I saw the stars all twinkling and a crescent moon. On the plains I heard a huge sacred white buffalo running. I yelled to the shadow and said, *Wanka, wanka!*

Why was I saying these words? Had they a meaning? Then I recognized it. It meant Manitou in the Plains Indian tongue, Wankatonka. Then I said, "Great Father Manitou, help me. I am afraid of the demigods."

Then a voice spoke to me from above and said, "I have tested you with my shadow. I have been with you and when I left you were afraid. All demigods fear me. Do not be afraid of them. I will give you a sign.

"Here I give you two colours, one dark blue to represent night, one light blue to represent day. Take this material like the finest silk. That represents day and night. Use these two colours or make anything with them, a shirt, a bag, a charm. With this I shall protect you always against demigods and all sorcery."

That dream left a strong impression upon me. Afterwards I started to do art and paint legends without fear of offending my ancestral spirits.

THE SHAKING TENT RITES OF THE OJIBWAY INDIANS AND CONJURING

The Ojibway Indians had what we call a jeesekun, a shaking tent, or wigwam, where a medicine man does conjuring. There were two kinds of shaking tents. One had its power from the water, the other from the wind or earth. Some Ojibway built their shaking tent in the water, in order to receive power from it. Eight poles were cut and placed in a circle, and each pole was driven about two feet into the ground to keep the tent firm. Two hoops were placed inside the wigwam to keep the poles in position and would be covered with deer hide, birchbark or canvas. Rattles of tin or caribou hoof were placed inside to make a rattling noise.

All the Ojibway would gather and sit in a circle facing the shaking tent. This took place at night. The conjurer would disrobe, have his hands tied up and crawl inside the wigwam. He would not speak but would have one Indian, or all, start asking questions, whatever each one wished to know. As the conjurer crawled inside, the tent itself began to shake and the rattles were heard. The Ojibway believe a medicine wind blows from heaven in the tent and that is how it shakes. All the dogs tied close by began to yelp and were afraid but the people were not, for it does not affect human beings. What come into the wigwam to sing or talk are the water god Misshipeshu and other spirits of bears, serpents and animals, thunderbirds, the evil Windigo, the morning star, the sky, water, earth, sun and moon, also female and male sex organs. Each speaks in his own language but we have an interpreter whom we call Mikkinnuk, a small turtle who is the Devil himself, who interprets for all these beings. So let it be known now and then remain a secret; it is the Devil himself who is the interpreter.

The Ojibway were given this shaking tent to do both good and evil. A lot of people of the Ojibway tribe used this conjuring tent to conjure people but a lot also used it to cure people, to find lost things, to defend the people from evil sorcerers, or bad medicine-men, and to know about the future.

To give you a better idea, I will give you examples of the questions asked.

First question: "How is my friend doing who is two hundred miles away? Is he sick or all right? I am worried."

As I said, we have an interpreter, Mikkinnuk. According to a fable we read in the white man's schools, the turtle beat the rabbit in a race. This I believe to be true. The Ojibway believe that when the interpreter is asked to find out about the friend who is two hundred miles away, this turtle goes to that village and back again in a matter of four minutes. Then he will say, "Everything is fine. No one is sick," and that the friend is having a powwow. Afterwards the friend is asked if this is true and will say that there really was a powwow at that time. Four minutes to travel two hundred miles and return is really travelling. Perhaps the turtle did beat the rabbit after all.

Second question: When the Ojibway of Lake Nipigon were travelling on the portages of the Nipigon River one Indian lost a packsack full of goods. There were about fifteen people there at the time. It was near Pine Portage on the Nipigon River, and after doing some fall shopping at the Hudson's Bay or McKirdy's store this man lost one packsack. He was afraid that someone might have stolen it but did not want to blame anyone until he was sure, so he went to a conjurer who could perform the shaking tent rite and asked his assistance to find the lost packsack. He was told by the conjurer to erect a wigwam and that he would perform the ceremony that evening.

Later that evening when the conjurer started his performance Mikkinnuk told the Indians, including the owner of the packsack, that it was safe three portages down the river, that no one had tried to steal it but that it had been misplaced by the owner. "But," said Mikkinnuk, "although I went to the place where the packsack is and tried to bring it back, it was too heavy for me to carry as I am only a small turtle. So go early in the morning and you will find it at the place I mentioned." Sure enough it was there.

The conjurer had to perform this tent rite all his life, for the power lasted always. Once an Indian started using this for evil ways he could never quit, for he was a slave to the tent and had to do what he was told or the spirits would go against him. If the conjurer were offered some goods or money and asked by an Indian to harm his enemy, he had to perform this wigwam ceremony.

Often conjurers conjured Indians over family quarrels. This was very bad but it had to be done. As I said, if the conjurer did not do the things he was asked, the evil spirits that helped him perform and gave him power would turn against him. There were women conjurers, too, who had power to perform the shaking tent, as well as good conjurers who used the tent to help people against evil conjurers.

Now I wish to explain what the Indian dreams when he or she is given the power to perform the tent rite.

One old Ojibway lady said, "In my early years, when I was sixteen, I went into the great forest to fast. I did not eat for seven days. The spirits

Mikkinnuk the Turtle and the Shaking Tent

spoke to me in my medicine dream and said that I would perform six shaking tents at the same time and that these would be used for good, to help my people against evil conjurers. But," said the lady, "I was told I had to pass a test. I did not know what it was. I was taken to a big pit full of evil serpents who looked very fierce and had a lot of teeth. I was told to jump into this hole. I was afraid but I gave in, anyway. If I was to be powerful I had to do what I was asked. I jumped into this hole. When I landed at the bottom there were no snakes but I was inside a shaking tent. As I sat there I felt power in me. That was my dream."

One time about forty years ago she was asked to perform the shaking tents but was unable to perform the whole six as she was too old, and as a conjurer grows old his power leaves him little by little. She said, "When I was twenty years old I performed six tents. In each of the first two I put one of my shoes, in each of the second two one of my mitts, my medicine bags in the fifth and myself in the sixth. Then all began to shake at the same time. When I was forty, two left me. When I was forty-five years old another left me. When I was fifty yet another left me, and when I was sixty-five years old all left me. Now I could perform no more magic for my power was gone. But I am not sorry. I am glad. I have helped a lot of people, doing good and using my powers to protect them from evil. I was known by all the Ojibway throughout the district of Thunder Bay to be powerful for good."

One Ojibway medicine-man said this, "When I was given the power to perform the shaking tent I saw the Devil himself. I was not afraid. He told me I was to be a very powerful conjurer. He promised me I would be considered a god by the Ojibway and that I would be known from Lake Nipigon to Red River, Manitoba, and up to the far north. But I had to pass a test. I submitted to the test. The Devil told me to disrobe and stand naked and to bend down showing my ass to him, and he blew into my rectum. I felt power going through me and coming out of my mouth and I cannot describe how it felt when he blew. After it was all over I was told that I was now a full-fledged conjurer, and that I am now."

He died fifteen years ago, about ninety years old, but all his power had then left him. He had to pay heavily, however, for the power that was given to him, for he lost his very soul for ever.

My mother's grandfather was conjured into a shaking tent some fifty-five years ago at Lake Helen at Nipigon, Ontario. This Indian, whom we shall call John, was walking on the beach of Lake Helen when suddenly he felt tired and sleepy and sat upon a rock to rest. Something was about to happen to him; whether it was a dream or not, I do not know.

John saw a very young man coming in his direction carrying a medicine pipe decorated in the very best style. He asked him to smoke the pipe; John accepted the offer and was told to follow. As he followed the young man down the road he noticed he was now at Hurkett, Ontario.

Guarding the doorway of a shaking tent that was about to be conjured lay two huge water demi-gods, growling and showing their teeth. At the top of the tent opening stood some watching thunder-birds. John could not escape, for every passage was blocked. Then he heard the voice of two Indian women whom he knew, Big Sun and Big Bullet. The women said to the conjurer, "Now that we have John in the tent, let us give the word to fix him up for good. For he is always mocking us and saying bad things to us and that is why we asked you to conjure him." The conjurer said what he thought about the women for interfering, adding that the time for conjuring the Indian was up and that it had been a long time since he left his body.

John spoke to the thunderbirds who guarded

the top of the door. "O great thunderbirds, help me, remember me. I am your medicine dream. Help me to get out of here." The thunderbirds moved aside and John went out of the tent. He next remembered facing the lake, wondering if this was all a dream or if he had been conjured as he believed.

If John had not had a medicine-bird dream he would have been conjured and would have been dead. Those who found him would never have known what actually took place and would have thought he had died of natural causes.

This is the history, as told orally to me, of my direct ancestor Little Grouse, who first erected the offering rocks at Lake Nipigon three hundred or more years ago. After Little Grouse erected the offering rocks he became a man of great medicine knowledge and was a conjurer, or sorcerer, skilled in the Ojibway rites. Although feared, he never did harm to any one, even though his knowledge was great and he had the power to fight back good and hard.

One winter at Hurkett, Ontario, there lived another great sorcerer, or medicine-man, called Lynx Paw in the Ojibway tongue. Having heard of the power Little Grouse had, he felt that he should challenge it. Lynx Paw told his closest companion that this winter Little Grouse should suffer great hunger, for no animal would enter his wooden traps nor would he kill any moose. He was right.

Little Grouse knew what had happened but did not take revenge yet. Finally Lynx Paw went further. Then Little Grouse said to his people, who suffered with him, "I have never used my powers for wrong. I have tried to live in good faith. Revenge is a hard word, but one ought not to be bothered when one has done no harm. The law of the demigods states that no sorcerer or medicine-man shall ever use his powers on anyone without cause, or the spirits will turn against him.

I never bothered Lynx Paw, so now, according to our law and beliefs, I will take my revenge and his name shall ᴅe cleared from the earth."

That summer, around June, Lynx Paw and his many followers, for he was a great medicine-man, were on their way to the summer dances up Black Sturgeon River, to one of the high falls that had a sandy beach. All started getting ready for the dances. When they were fully absorbed in the rites the falls stopped. The waters stopped running. The Indians in fear and amazement looked up to see a great serpent with teeth staring at them at the top of the falls. Lynx Paw and his fellows grabbed their canoes and ran. Before reaching the mouth of the river Lynx Paw died with blood pouring from his mouth and eyes.

The wrong he did to my ancestor was revenged according to the law. For no man shall do evil unprovoked, or his guardians will go against him and leave him without help.

One Ojibway woman of the Red Lake area came up to me in the street and told me that she wanted to speak to me. Being a stranger, she thought she would frighten me. She made a mistake in approaching me.

She said, "I have heard about your sorcery and medicine knowledge."

I have none. I asked, "What did you hear?"

She said that my name was Copper Thunderbird, a very strong name for an Indian to have unless he was powerful. Then she told me, "I am powerful, too. Also I have known the thunderbirds. Let us try our sorcery to see who is the stronger."

Then I said to her, "Look, lady, whoever you are or feel you are. Drunk, you may feel like a demigoddess. Listen to what I have to tell you. Know that I don't fear you, for you are not God. Only God knows what death or sickness will fall upon me, not you who are full of pride, yet lowly. You are an old lady who should be advanced in wisdom.

Thunderbirds

ᐃᓇᖅᑕᐅᑕᐸᕆᓕ

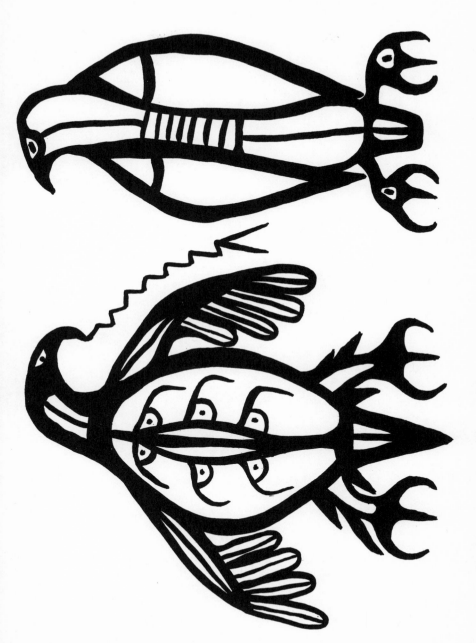

Compared with you I am young, like a son who knows nothing. We are told to respect all our elders, for it is the law of the Ojibway, but for you I have no respect. All you do is put fear into the Indians through sorcery, about which you know only what you have read. The law of our ancestors concerning sorcery teaches that no Indian shall threaten any of his own race with sorcery without a cause. If that person does, the law states that the demigods on his or her side shall devour or go against that person, and that teaching I follow."

As I finished saying this she looked at me and said, "Indeed, you are a man with great knowledge of the ways of our ancestors."

"Yes," I said, "and if I believe I will get sick my mind will make me sick. But if I don't believe I will never be bothered with your threats."

"Indeed, you are right," said this lady.

Today I see her often. She has a great respect for me and I in return respect her. She used to make a lot of people scared.

WINDIGO
AND OTHER
BAD LUCK STORIES
AND
DEATH BELIEFS

The Ojibway and Cree Indians have many legends of Windigo, the evil spirit who grows to a great height and eats human flesh. If an Ojibway had evil dreams of Windigo at the time of fasting, he would from time to time turn into Windigo so that the demon might satisfy his great hunger for human flesh. The Windigo lives up north and is accompanied by a blizzard of pouring snow and ice. When Windigo came upon an Indian village he would yell a mighty yell. All who heard this voice for miles around dropped to the ground in a fainting condition.

An Indian up north while fasting one time had bad dreams of Windigo. The evil spirit came to him disguised as a good spirit and promised a lot of things to the poor Indian, who forgot about his dream for he was just a boy of fourteen. One day, when this man was thirty years old and un-married, he felt a great hunger come upon him. He tried to appease his hunger on moose meat and deer but was unable to satisfy his craving for more.

That night the Indian felt as if he were getting big. His very clothes began to rip. Finally he passed out and did not remember any more. Then the Indian was changed into Windigo, so tall that his head reached the low-flying clouds. His one idea was to eat and satisfy his great hunger. Now Windigo entered into the unconscious Indian who began to eat all that his stomach could hold, until he was full. Then he started for home. As the

Indian got to his lonely home where he lived by himself and the snow covered his tracks, he returned to his human form and Windigo's spirit went away. The Indian then awoke in his tent and felt his hunger had left him but did not remember what took place. He forgot it as if it were a bad dream and went back to what he was doing until, after some time, again his great hunger would return.

All the Indian tribes of the northern part of Canada were afraid of Windigo. One time the Ojibway asked for protection against this evil spirit. The Great Manitou answered their plea and sent a guardian to them. The Great Spirit, through a medicine dream, told Kitchinikkoo, or Big Goose, to change himself from his human form into a mighty giant called Missahba, in the same manner as Windigo came to the northern Indian. Big Goose felt Windigo was about to come among them again and told his people, the Ojibway, to prepare great amounts of goose oil. He said, "Windigo will come but do not be afraid, for I will battle with him to the end and have his spirit put away."

One day the Indian up north again felt his great hunger come upon him and changed into Windigo. This time he was even mightier and his head reached the clouds. The Indians felt Windigo's presence and up on the far horizon saw two blazes like two suns, which were the eyes of Windigo. His step was heard by all. The very earth trembled. All the Indians were afraid, but Big Goose told them not to be, saying, "I will defend you, my people."

"How can a small human defend an entire nation of Ojibway and Crees against Windigo whose head touches the clouds?"

"Trust me," said Big Goose and he added, "Windigo's voice will be even mightier this time. Many of you will fall down at the sound of the mighty yell, but I will make you all well again."

Then Windigo's voice was heard. Everyone fell

83

to the ground. Only one person was still upright, walking to meet Windigo, and that was Big Goose himself. At each step he was getting bigger until his head touched the very clouds, for he was now Missahba the giant. As the two met a big battle took place. Trees were used as clubs, mountains were levelled, the ice on the Great Lakes was broken. But Windigo was killed and his spirit put away.

Big Goose returned to his normal feelings and his human-size body feeling very cold and icy, for he had inhaled the bad ice of Windigo during the fight and now felt it inside his body. The goose oil that was prepared in advance was used by Kitchinikkoo to throw up the bad ice. Afterwards all the Ojibway were restored in the same manner and woke up. The Ojibway gave great thanks to the Great Manitou for giving them a protector to defend them against this evil spirit. From that day until now Windigo never had to be feared, for he was destroyed forever.

A shrew, or small mouse, found lying dead on its back is believed by the Ojibway to bring bad luck. The shrew is also believed to be a messenger of death. Also there is a brown bird, about the size of a robin, who is considered bad luck and who sits and sings his death song in one place. This lasts all summer, both day and night. Again, if a fox barks near your home or at your tent or fire, this, too, is considered an omen of death.

The robin is respected among the Ojibway, for the robin is understood to say in Indian, *Neeshewukjeebeyuk,* which means "two dead persons." Legend has it that at one time the Ojibway lost two young boys who died in the great forest. The parents were seated by the fire broken-hearted at their loss, when a robin was noticed flying back and forth from tree to tree singing this song. The father spoke to the wife, "Listen to the robin. I can understand what it is singing. Can you? It is giving us a message, 'Two dead persons.' Let us follow the robin." They did and found their two small boys in a stump, dead for a long time. This is why the robin is respected.

One summer when my ancestor Little Grouse was getting old and his days were not long, he was going down the Nipigon River on a very stormy day. The thunderbirds were really making a lot of noise down the river. Finally it stopped and the sun began to come out. When he reached a certain place thunder was heard again. He looked in amazement to see a huge, big Misshipeshu with remains of bits of meat and bones on top of the rocks. Thinking it was a sign of some misfortune he went on his way. This foretold his death, for one year later my ancestor died.

At Nipigon Bay in early spring an Ojibway Indian was walking on the ice. Looking at the setting sun casting its shadows upon the cliffs, he saw the faces of the Maymaygwaysiwuk in all the cracks of the cliff walls, singing. This was a bad omen that foretold his death that summer by sickness.

I was told what was supposed to have taken place years ago at Squaw Bay Mission at Fort William. One clear night a ball of fire was seen coming toward the village from the Mount McKay mountains. It travelled in mid-air until it reached the first house. Then it went to every building and exploded in every smoke pipe. This sign was to foretell a great epidemic of smallpox that pretty nearly wiped out all the Ojibway there, so many died. From the few that remained are descended the present Ojibway Indians of Fort William.

One clear winter night in another area a human yell was heard in the sky from the east and within seconds was heard in the west. The Indians knew to whom the yell belonged: it was the human-like, living skeleton, called Paakuk, who has roamed the skies and flown over the earth since the dawn of history because of the wrong he did by committing the first sorcery murder among the Ojibway.

To hear his yell without fear foretold long life, but to fear meant death. To smell his smell foretold sickness. That year all the Ojibway in that area smelled Paakuk, which was a bad sign, for smallpox took all lives a year later. The Ojibway believe that Paakuk will never stop flying until the end of the world. Ojibway Christians believe that it is Cain who flies for ever and that God gave him this punishment for killing Abel.

Paakuk is known to fly very fast. One second his mournful cry is heard in the skies in the east, the next second in the east-west, the next second in the west. It is not often that Paakuk is heard. At James Bay, Ontario, an old Indian lady told me her grandmother heard a mournful yell in the tree tops. It was Paakuk, asking to be set loose. "When my grandmother, who was sixteen then," said this lady, "saw Paakuk stuck between two trees, he asked her to pry him loose, offering in return a ripe old age. She climbed the tree and freed him. As she looked upon him a sound was heard, then Paakuk disappeared beyond the horizon. She died at the age of one hundred and two years."

THE GREAT CONJURERS AND WARRIORS OF THE MIGHTY OJIBWAY

The ancestors of my direct ancestor Little Grouse were Assiniboine, or Stony Indians of the Canadian Plains, his totem being the great grizzly bear of the Plains, and today the totem of my grandfather, Moses Nanakonagos of Beardmore, is the same.

All Ojibway Indians had totems of animals and fish and birds, and all the Ojibway who had the same totem were very closely related. No matter if you had never seen the person, if he or she had the same totem then they were your relative. No one ever married anybody with the same totem. This was the custom of the Ojibway.

About forty-five years ago or more the Hudson's Bay Company gathered all the Indians together to celebrate a centennial year. My grandfather painted his totem on his wigwam, according to the custom of the Plains. He noticed animal totems similar to his painted on other wigwams. Later an old Stony elder asked who was the Ojibway who had the grizzly bear totem. Although they had never met as relatives, they embraced one another in an Indian greeting, and with the help of an interpreter declared that they were related through the totem. Then my grandfather explained the history of this relationship as follows.

During the wars among the Indians the Ojibway, being a great nation to be feared, went into the plains in the land of the Stonies to fight. The Ojibway passed a law that if a full-scale battle were fought and all the enemy killed, any surviving children should not be killed or mistreated but brought back to be adopted as children of the Ojibway.

Two children were brought back, brothers about ten years old or younger. Those were my ancestors on my mother's side. When the younger was fifteen he died. The other lived with my people at Lake Nipigon, or in the Thunder Bay area. He married an Ojibway woman and lived as an Ojibway, not recalling his original tongue or land. Perhaps his adopted parents treated him as one of their own tribesmen. One of his children was the man that I mentioned, Little Grouse.

The adoption of Plains Indian children into the Ojibway tribes might have inspired their beliefs in their Ojibway adopted parents, if some were old enough to know those of their true parents. Perhaps this is one reason some rock paintings show Plains' influence.

The great Ojibway also fought to defend our country, Ontario, the place we loved. We, the Ojibway, fought the People of the Long Houses, the great Nadawa. We always wanted to live in peace but we were for ever being pestered by other tribes and we did what was right. It is said that the People of the Long Houses were the fighting tribe, but we drove all the tribes out of Ontario and our name, the Ojibway, is still feared.

There was a tribe of Indians called Ojijakoonsuk who were very troublesome, although they never hurt or killed anyone, but they had a habit of stealing whatever they got their hands on. Sometimes they would try to steal young women for wives. At times they succeeded. They are believed to have lived at Albany. These Indians were short and heavy, about four and half to five feet tall. In their tribe they had a chief who was a troublemaker. This chief advised all his men to go among the Ojibway and steal and make trouble. The Ojibway finally laid down the law and made them stop these troublesome habits and showed them that the Ojibway word was to be obeyed, or they

Thunderbird, Loon Totem and Evil Fish

would kill all their tribe, sparing no one. From that day no Ojijakoons ever bothered the Ojibway again, for the Ojibway were their masters and the law of the Ojibway had to be respected.

A story is based upon a tribe of Ojibway Indians and a tribe of Long House People known as the Noduweck. This occurred in the Great Lakes area. This story is written as it happened. One day the chief of the Noduweck, Medicine Turtle, said to his people, "I am going on a long journey to visit the land of the Ojibway and to see their chief, Red Bird. I go to challenge Red Bird to a contest of strength."

One night Red Bird awoke from sleep and went outside. Summoning his people to him, he said, "My people, there will be a visitor to our village in three weeks."

During that time the Noduweck tribe were on a war party against a different village of Indians. They camped on an island for two nights. During these two nights Medicine Turtle dreamed that he was defeated by a red bird, whom he knew to be the Ojibway Indian chief. When he awoke he wondered how he could ever be defeated when only he had medicine powers, so he changed his plans and decided to go to Red Bird immediately to see how strong his medicine was. He told his people to wait on the island till he returned. Before leaving, Medicine Turtle told them, "I will go there alone to show that I am not a coward." He was not afraid to travel alone because he was a great medicine-man. Medicine Turtle put his canoe to water and started out on his mission.

The day before Medicine Turtle was to reach Red Bird's camp Red Bird dreamed of his arrival. He awoke and told his people, "Tomorrow at noon our visitor will arrive and he will come through the bend of the lake." Just around noon the dogs started barking, when suddenly around a bend of the lake came into view a canoe with a lone person on board.

Red Bird stood on shore and watched the canoe come closer to the camp. He knew by the designs on the canoe and by the colours of the feathers on the chief's bonnet exactly where he had come from. The dogs barked and boys and girls threw rocks at the visitor. Medicine Turtle spoke: "I have journeyed many miles. Is this the welcome that I receive?"

Red Bird told his people to stop their way of welcoming the visitor and said, "I am Red Bird, chief of the Ojibway Indians, whom you seek. What brings you so far from your hunting grounds and for what reason are you here?"

Medicine Turtle replied, "I am tired from my journey. I need rest."

Red Bird told two of his people to give their visitor a wigwam. After he was fed he rested for the night.

Next morning Red Bird summoned the visitor. "I know that you have not come here in peace. After you have finished what you came to do, go back to your country and return here no more."

First they smoked from the medicine pipe, or calumet. Later on Medicine Turtle said, "Red Bird, I dreamed of being defeated by a red bird in a small contest to match medicine powers, and I am here to prove that my medicine is stronger than yours."

First they did conjuring. Medicine Turtle had four shaking tents in which he thought he had done more than Red Bird. Red Bird had six shaking tents and won on that.

Then Medicine Turtle told Red Bird's people, "Look over there. You will see a big snake with horns, the protector of my people, the Noduweck."

Now Red Bird spoke: "Look over there, Noduweck. See the thunderbirds in the sky. They are after your protector." The big snake was killed. Red Bird spoke again. "Medicine Turtle, you have been defeated a second time. It is no use for you to continue."

Medicine Turtle replied, "What I really came here for is to beat your magic power in a personal contest. If I beat you will you surrender your people to mine?"

Red Bird's only answer was, "If you win." Red Bird spoke again. "What sort of contest do you, Medicine Turtle, wish to challenge me to?"

Medicine Turtle pointed to a shoal out on the lake as far as the naked eye could see. "Now," said Medicine Turtle, "with this one arrow I will fire towards the shoal and we will go there later to see how deeply the arrow has been embedded in the rock." When they went to the shoal they saw that about nineteen inches of the two-foot arrow was embedded in rock. After the two chiefs returned to shore Medicine Turtle said, "Now it is your turn, Red Bird, show me how strong your medicine powers are."

"Not with an arrow but this feather," Red Bird replied, plucking it from his bonnet, "I will prove to you, Medicine Turtle, how strong my medicine powers are." Red Bird placed the feather on his bowstring and fired.

Upon reaching the shoal they found the feather one quarter-inch from the arrow shot by Medicine Turtle. The feather could barely be seen sticking out of the solid rock. As in his dream, Medicine Turtle was defeated. He left the Ojibway Indians in shame but full of thoughts of revenge.

Medicine Turtle told his warriors, "Tonight I will return to Red Bird's camp but this time I will not be alone. We will attack the Ojibway camp and massacre them all. Red Bird will pay for beating me."

Meanwhile, back at Red Bird's camp, Red Bird spoke to all his people. "Tonight many canoes will come. Medicine Turtle will return here with many warriors to massacre our people in revenge for his defeat against me. My people, tonight we will leave everything as it is now. The fires will continue to burn. We will go to an island five miles from here and wait there until the attack is over."

One old woman, Nokomis, wanted to stay in camp. She said, "I will not leave my wigwam. I will not leave here. Nobody will tell me what to do, not even you, Red Bird, will make me leave here."

Red Bird tried to reason with the woman and told her she would be killed by Medicine Turtle if she stayed in camp, but in vain. The woman suffered from a touch of mental illness. Before Red Bird left camp he told her, "Before we leave you alone here I will leave you one birchbark canoe, in case you should change your mind and decide to come."

Red Bird and all his people left camp and headed for the island five miles away. When they reached the island they rested, but no fires were made. During the night, all of a sudden, they saw flames and heard war whoops. They knew that Medicine Turtle had reached their camp. Red Bird wondered about the woman he had left in camp. They heard screams and sounds of torture and Red Bird knew it was her voice. Nokomis had been killed by the Noduweck, but before being killed she had told Medicine Turtle where Red Bird had gone with his people. Medicine Turtle told his warriors, "We will go to this island where Red Bird and his people are and we will kill every last one."

Meanwhile, back at the island, a little boy was playing by the shore. Suddenly he felt a foreboding of trouble. He ran to camp and told Red Bird, "Red Bird, Red Bird, I have a feeling that we will be attacked by enemy warriors."

"Don't be afraid, for no one knows where we are. It is only your imagination."

During the next night all was quiet. The waters were calm and smooth like glass. Suddenly Red Bird's dog Noëdin started growling. In English Noëdin means wind (like "The wind blows," not "Did you wind the clock?"). Red Bird said to his warriors, "Noëdin expects trouble, or visitors to the island." Red Bird then told his warriors to prepare for battle and commanded them also to be quiet. (All Indian children were taught from birth not to cry. This was done so that the babies' crying would not give the camp away to the enemy.)

Suddenly Red Bird heard splashing sounds and knew they were the noise of canoes. He could just see the outlines of many canoes but could not tell to whom they belonged. Upon reaching the shore Medicine Turtle said, "This is the island that the squaw told us Red Bird was on, but he is not here. Perhaps she told us a lie." As they were leaving, Red Bird's dog Noëdin started growling. Medicine Turtle heard and said, "They are here. Attack." War whoops were heard and a battle began.

The battle lasted for many hours. Finally it was over. Red Bird lost many of his brave warriors, but the Noduweck lost all except Medicine Turtle, who was spared for a reason. Red Bird asked Medicine Turtle how he had known where to find him, and Medicine Turtle told Red Bird where he got his information.

"Now, Medicine Turtle," said Red Bird, "I have spared you so that you can return to your people and tell them of your experiences here. And if you ever come to our land again we will kill all your people. Now go. Be on your way." And Medicine Turtle was given a canoe to travel with.

Red Bird and his remaining warriors and people returned to their original camping grounds and found everything smashed and all the wigwams burned to the ground. One of his warriors who was named Maungoose, Little Loon, came to Red Bird almost in tears and said, "Red Bird, come and see what they have done to Nokomis." Red Bird went with Little Loon and his people followed.

What Red Bird and his people saw will be explained in the most proper and decent way possible. There was a six-foot pole stuck into the ground. On this pole was Nokomis; she had been tortured and killed in the same fashion as any person would barbecue a pig or other animal.

"For this awful and brutal torture, my people," said Red Bird, "all Noduweck shall pay, and I will not rest until this memory is washed away from my mind."

It started snowing. It began to turn cold and the ground and the lakes froze. Then the winter had passed and the snow melted away. Finally the lakes were open once again and canoes were put to water.

Two canoes of Ojibway Indians went to hunt on a certain lake and they were gone for four days. On their way back to camp with what they had caught they passed an island. Suddenly one warrior, Bear Paw, noticed someone moving along the island's shore. Bear Paw told his people to stop: "Let's go and see who it is."

They paddled towards the island and saw that it was an Indian fishing along the shore. He was as naked as on the day he was born. Bear Paw yelled to the Indian who was stooping down, "Hey, who are you? Are you lost and where are you from?"

When he lifted his head they recognized him as Medicine Turtle, the leader who killed Nokomis, and they shot arrows into his body.

Before shooting, Bear Paw said, "Medicine Turtle, you will now pay for your crime and for your part in the torture of Nokomis. Your fighting days are over."

Medicine Turtle begged for mercy.

Bear Paw said, "The only mercy is to kill you now, because if we were to take you back to Red Bird he would give you a more severe torture than you gave to Nokomis."

So Medicine Turtle roamed no more.

Many years later, when Red Bird was growing old and feeble, he decided that he should return to visit relatives in Fort Hope. He travelled by water. On his way he met an Indian named Potan, who travelled with him to Fort Hope. Upon reaching Fort Hope, Red Bird and his companions were greeted by relatives of Red Bird, who told them of an evil medicine-man who lived alone in their midst and had killed many of his people for reasons unknown. Red Bird was told also to watch how he spoke and acted, for it was very easy to arouse this man's anger. The chief was warned that the evil conjurer would welcome a visitor, whether friend or stranger. He would then light his pipe and as long as the tobacco burned in his pipe the visitor was allowed to remain in his wigwam, but if the visitor did not leave after the tobacco was all burned he would be angry and kill him by black magic. Red Bird decided to visit this evil conjurer and see how strong his medicine powers were.

Red Bird entered the wigwam of the evil conjurer. He was greeted and sat down to talk. When the tobacco was all burned Red Bird did not leave. The medicine-man refilled his pipe a second time. Again, when the tobacco was all burned Red Bird still remained seated. The evil conjurer was now filled with great anger but he also sensed that this visitor was different from other visitors and knew now that Red Bird, too, was a man with great medicine powers.

The evil conjurer said to Red Bird, "You who are still in my wigwam after being warned twice to leave must also be a medicine-man and a conjurer. Now we will see which of us has stronger powers. Show me what you can do."

Red Bird reached into his buckskin coat and pulled out a piece of deer hide that he hung up in the doorway of the wigwam. Next Red Bird shot an arrow towards the deer hide. Blood came pouring out. The evil conjurer in his turn shot an arrow towards the deer hide but nothing happened; the arrow only went through it. The evil conjurer was defeated.

"Now it is your turn," said Red Bird.

The evil conjurer dug into his medicine bag

and brought out a stone that was as hard as the Rock of Gibraltar. He placed the rock between his two hands and ground part of the stone to the fineness of sand. Red Bird took what was left of the stone and with one hand shattered it into many fine pieces. The evil conjurer was defeated for the second time. But he never gave up.

Red Bird left the wigwam and continued his visits to different far-off places. As Red Bird and Potan paddled on their way, Red Bird heard a humming and a shrieking sound of something coming very fast behind them. Potan made as if to look back, but Red Bird said, "Don't look back, Potan, whatever you do."

As the mysterious noise came closer and closer Red Bird and Potan kept paddling. Light began to shine on either side of them. Red Bird lifted his paddle, as the sound was really close, and hit something solid. After that the sound stopped, the light went out and there was a splashing noise. They stopped the canoe and looked back. There beside the canoe was a black bat with blood pouring from the corner of its mouth. It swam around and around the surface of the water until it died. Red Bird and Potan continued their journey.

The next summer Red Bird returned to Fort Hope. While visiting his relatives he noticed that the wigwam of the evil conjurer was nowhere in sight. Red Bird asked one of his relatives where the evil conjurer was, and was told that he had died the same day that he and Potan had left the previous summer. He had been found dead outside his tent with the blood pouring from the corner of his mouth, and his people had no idea what had happened. Then Red Bird knew what had happened. The evil conjurer had been defeated for the third and last time.

Afterwards Red Bird went to Longlac to visit Wahsahkeezhik, or Bright Sky, who had returned from the dead. And from him he learned how to pray. Before that his medicine-power guardians had told him that if he continued his magic prac-

98

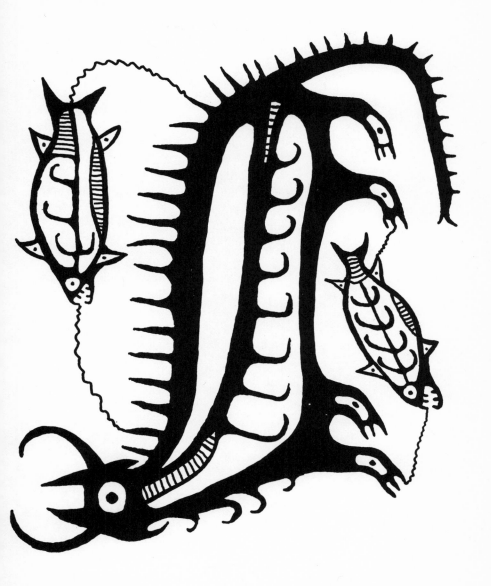

tices he would live to be a hundred years old. But
Red Bird had made up his mind to leave his medicine powers and pray to God as he was told to do
by Wahsahkeezhik. He continued his praying until
he died at the age of seventy-five, twenty-five years
short of the life he would have lived if he had still
practised his medicine-power belief.

So ends our story of a great Ojibway chief Red
Bird, Misskubinneshee in Ojibway, and of his
many experiences and exploits.

THE WHITE MAN'S
COMING TO
THE NIPIGON AREA

Many years ago a medicine-man of the Lake Nipigon Indians told his people that he was inspired by a dream of a white loon that would appear on the Nipigon River cliffs. This sign would foretell the proportion of white men to Indians, depending on which direction the white loon faced. If the loon faced Lake Nipigon, the mother waters, this would mean there would be many Indians and fewer white men, but if the loon faced Nipigon, Ontario, the reverse would be true. I understand the white loon faced Nipigon, and today the Indians are outnumbered by the white men.

When the Ojibway first saw a plane with wings they believed it was a huge dragonfly. Ojibway Indians at Long Lake did not know what the train was, although they had seen the white men building a railroad track, the CNR branch line from Port Arthur to Longlac. Some time later, while Ojibway children were swimming by the shores of Kenogamishish Lake near Geraldton, they heard their first train blow and ran crying and yelling all the way from the shore into the birchbark wigwams, thinking that Windigo was after them.

An Ojibway elder told me this tale. Many years ago there lived a tribe of Ojibway Indians at Lake Helen at Nipigon. The treaty payment to them was just in its early years, as this was their third summer payment. I was told that the agent who used to pay the treaty moneys travelled by canoe from Lake Superior to pay these Ojibway at Lake Helen at Nipigon.

At this time the Indians were given some fire-water, a gift from the ruling queen of England, and told that they should use it for medical reasons. They were also told of its effects if too much were taken. According to the story, the head of each family—that would be the father—was given a small jug of firewater. Everyone was glad. Meantime the agent went on his way to Lake Superior until next treaty payment time. The Ojibway all got drunk on the whisky and, according to what I was told, a fight started between two cousins. One after another took part until they all started to fight. Having guns, they started to kill each other and burned their wigwams, children and dogs. Next day only a few remained alive.

This tragedy, I understand, was the reason the Indian could not get any liquor or firewater until now, for the Indian could not hold his drink and there are a few who cannot today. But viewed impartially, both the white and the Indian are the same. There are a lot of white people who get crazy drinking, just like the Indians. There are also Indians who can drink like our respectable white brothers. This is written not to criticize anyone but to tell what took place, for it was the harmful results of the white man's firewater that affected those primitive minds.

One time an old man told me that with his great power he would cause a big thunderstorm, because I refused to give him a dollar to buy a bottle of wine that he was supposed to offer to his demigod. In his anger, he said I would be so afraid of that thunder that I would get sick. I laughed at him. Two summers have passed. There were thunderstorms but not of his doing.

Idols are used by certain of the Ojibway people, who carve them out of cedar wood. Some are placed in a box or bag, some on a special stand. An Indian would offer firewater and tobacco to these idols.

My good friend Joe told me that once at a place around the Lake of the Woods area he saw a nice woman and went with her to her place. In return for the daughter's services, such as a date for a night, the old father wanted a bottle of whisky and would share that bottle. Later that night as the bottle was getting low, the old man spoke to my friend and said, "Now is the hour that I am going to offer my god a drink and I will place the bottle inside the shelf." On the shelf stood a carved idol. Then they all went to sleep.

Early next morning my friend, having a bad hangover, went secretly to that shelf, which had a small curtain, took the remaining whisky, drank it and returned to bed feeling better. Then later that morning they all woke up and the old man looked at the shelf and, seeing the bottle all empty, said, "Now, as I have said, he never fails to take my offering. My god took my drink."

Joe smiled to himself.

This story was told to my grandfather many years ago. One time, about two hundred years ago, in a place called Fort Hope, Ontario, there was a settlement of Ojibway Indians where there was a medicine-man who brought visitors from heaven to a huge wigwam shaped like a beaver house. Each spring the medicine-man would make this great wigwam and place holes in the top and sides, so that the great wind, if it blew on the top, would also blow out the sides.

After everyone was seated in a big circle about ten feet from the tent, the medicine-man inside would speak to the people outside and would say, "Now we shall have visitors again," and begin to pound his medicine drum. The great skies were clear and there was no wind.

All of a sudden a wind was heard to blow from the heavens and into the top of the wigwam, and from the holes on the sides came a refreshing breeze. In mid-air a rustle of people was heard but none were seen. Everyone was now looking and listening and from inside the wigwam people, men and women, were heard talking. The medicine-man inside spoke to the Indians without, saying, "Our visitors are here. Listen."

In those days the Indian people had never seen silk or satin, for everyone wore buckskin clothing. From the side of the opening on the wigwam appeared the finest silk in colours of red and blue and white. These the Ojibway Indians believed were the dresses of the visitors. The material came from the sides of the wigwam because the wind was blowing from heaven into the open top, forcing some of the clothing worn by the visitors to appear on the sides. After about an hour the drum was beaten again and the visitors were heard to leave. Everyone looked at the top, but nothing was to be seen and everything became quiet. Then the medicine-man appeared at the door of the wigwam and spoke to his people, "My people, you have again seen and heard our visitors from heaven. Next spring we shall invite them again."

The old lady who told this to my grandfather about fifty years ago was very old, she was ninety-nine. She said, "We were all surprised, not at the great magic but at the material we saw at that time. For everyone then wore buckskin clothing and no silk or satin was known to the Indians. Afterwards, when the Hudson's Bay Company came to us they brought with them the material we had previously seen and touched, that had blown out of the great medicine lodge."

OJIBWAY BELIEFS
ABOUT HEAVEN
AND
THE EFFECTS
OF CHRISTIAN BELIEFS

Superstition still lingers among the Ojibway. However much each depends on the Christian faith, there is still fear of the unknown. This will not always be so, but perhaps for another two generations or so.

Take a young man I know, who was taught at school, ever since he was old enough, to believe in the Christian beliefs. When he grew up he lived what he had been taught. On the other hand his brothers, who lived with the parents, were in some ways afraid of the supernatural. The father was an elder for thirty-five years, a Bible reader to the Indians and a good devoted Protestant, but had his fears of the demigods although he still preached the protection of God.

Some Ojibway people today become good Christians and forsake all Ojibway beliefs and fears and live a good life. On the other hand some Ojibway never accepted Christianity but follow the teachings of their ancestors. They also live a good life. But those who had no faith in either religion were the ones who lived in fear, for we must have faith in some good way of life.

Take myself. I am intelligent, I understand how the Christian religion came to be, how the Catholic Church was the only church established by Christ, and how it separated at the Reformation when a new Christian faith sprang up. On the other hand I know about my ancestral beliefs, their rights and wrongs, and I respect both teachings as sacred. I understand the loss I would have if I forsook my Indian religion for another and I serve both. Being intelligent I am not confused or lost, but if I were ignorant, or if I did not understand either of my faiths, then I believe I would be lost. For I would not know what it is all about.

About thirty years ago the Ojibway lady of Macdiarmid, Ontario, whose name was Elizabeth, whom I have already mentioned, lay very sick and dying in her bed. All her babies were crying, and as she lay there the Blessed Virgin appeared to her and said, "Elizabeth, my daughter, go back into your body. Go and look after your babies who are crying. If you should leave them there will be no one to look after them." She recovered from her sickness and lived, and her children grew to be adults. She died finally at the age of ninety years.

Many Ojibway who became devoted Christians of the Catholic faith believe it is the Devil himself who gives power to all conjurers. If the shaking tent is touched with a holy, blessed medal it stops. Also the medicine-man tells everyone to leave rosaries, crosses and medals at home and never to bring them to the ceremony, for they strongly affect the tent. The Protestant Bible affects the tent, too. Because of this proof a lot of Indians left conjuring alone and turned into good Christians.

At Poplar Lodge in Lake Nipigon, some seventy-five years ago, there lived Ojibway Indians some of whom became good Christians of the Catholic faith. There were some medicine-men, however, yet left in the area of Lake Nipigon who did not accept the white man's religion. At Grand Bay, Ontario, sixty miles across Lake Nipigon from Poplar Lodge, there lived seven powerful medicine-men who were evil and practised evil conjuring and bad medicine. The Ojibway feared these seven.

One time the seven conjurers made a powerful medicine arrow to fix up one of their enemies at Poplar Lodge, but instead of killing him the arrow affected twelve innocent people. This arrow is known by the Ojibway as the arrow of Bemooka-win. It is shot in the victim's direction and the power of the evil spirits is invoked. The arrow was made for an Ojibway Indian at Poplar Lodge who stole some traps from the Grand Bay Indians but, as I said, instead of affecting him alone, eleven others died very suddenly through a sickness not known to anyone except the Ojibway.

One of the eleven that died had a wife who was a devoted Christian and this sudden death brought a lot of sorrow to her heart. She did not forget, however, to pray to God and the saints and the Virgin of her faith, although the Ojibway at Poplar Lodge knew it was the seven evil conjurers who had done this to the people, through Bemookawin. This happened one early spring. The priest came to the Ojibway at Poplar Lodge that summer and this woman visited the priest and told what took place, how all twelve of the Ojibway including her husband had died through this evil work. Nearly in tears, she told this to the Indian-speaking French priest. For a while the priest was silent, then he asked three times if this was really what they believed and if what she said might be true. She replied, "Yes, Father."

"Very well," said the priest. "A human can hide a lot of things but to God nothing will ever be hidden, and if this really took place as you say, my child, then God will punish those who did this evil to their fellow Indians." And that was all.

The following winter news came from Grand Bay that the seven evil conjurers had died of flu, with severe colds and high temperatures. Those evil medicine-men all died that same year and the Indians then started to live in peace. Their bad influence had brought a lot of evil thinking to all and was the main reason why the Ojibway did not accept the Christian religion.

An old Ojibway woman of Gull Bay told me that once there was an old lady who was a Catholic very devoted to her faith, for which she had for-

saken all her ancestral beliefs. She lived a good life. When she died, according to the custom of Ojibway Catholics, her people prayed for three days and nights until she was buried, to pay their last respects. One evening during this time her daughter, who was full of sorrow for the loss of her mother, went outside, for it was a very clear night with a full moon.

As she was standing outside listening to the death hymns sung inside and looking up and wondering if her mother would go to any place called heaven, she heard the voices of many choirs in the air. Without fear but with gladness in her heart she gave thanks to the Godhead of the Christian faith. As she looked up to heaven, it was as if a door opened and through that hole a light shone toward earth. Then it closed. This sign foretold that she was to follow her mother about one year later.

Neegoomee is a fine Indian about fifty years old. I do not know what is in his mind, or if these claims are pure fantasy or imagination. What follows is what he has said to me.

"One time twelve years ago," he said, "I and my wife were trapping in the bush and had a little house with one small window, big enough for one bed, our supplies and a small stove. After we lay down to sleep one night I woke up to see little cherubs, or small angels, trying to pull the beaver meat out of the rack above the stove."

His wife told me her husband woke her up to look. "But," she said, "I did not see anything except the beaver meat." Neegoomee, however, was sure that he had seen this vision.

I do not know the explanation. I was told that at one time Neegoomee was a good Christian who never drank or did anything wrong and prayed at all times, but then he left his old ways to start drinking and never said his prayers. He now feels that he should start being a good Christian once more, as this vision means that he is required to practise Christianity again.

Neegoomee also told me this dream, which was very important in a way.

"One night as I was falling asleep," said Neegoomee, "behold, the sun itself began to come down from the sky right to the earth where I stood. I was not afraid.

"The sun said, 'Come, I will take you up to heaven.'

"I went and at the top there were choirs of angels and twelve books concerning all the religions of the earth. The Catholic and the Protestant scriptures were combined into one book. This dream means that all faiths, including Buddhism, Islam and so on, are related closely to the Catholic faith. I wanted to sing a song or a hymn, but an angel told me not to yet. I was also told that the Christian Godhead is a Catholic."

I do not write this in support of any faith or belief or teachings but only as it was told to me, and because it was an Ojibway Indian that told me and I felt that his dream should be recorded in this book with respect.

Ojibway belief states that no Indian can enter the happy hunting ground unless he is small. One Ojibway Indian medicine-man studied for years how a person might enter the great heavens. In a medicine dream he dreamed that he was going to heaven on a big ladder. It was tiring and very hard to climb. Finally he reached the very top. When he got there he saw a small hole and tried to fit his head in but was unable to do so, for his head was too big. He tried his finger and it fitted but he was unable to bring the rest of his body through. Finally he looked into the hole. It was very bright and clear on the other side. Then, knowing it was useless, he came down again. Next day he told the people about his medicine dream and said, "When a person dies he or she becomes very small and fits into the small hole in the heavens. But if they are alive or in a human form a person cannot fit into this hole, for it is very hard for anyone to go to heaven unless he is dead."

Another time this old elder dreamed he went to the far south to a place known to the Ojibway, where Indians go after they die. Upon getting there he saw Indians who had been dead a long time having a great feast of mushrooms and was offered some. But he did not accept the offer. The Indian believed that if he did eat he would not return to his human form or the place where he fell asleep.

The Ojibway believe that some part of the body goes out of it in dreams.

Another Ojibway belief is that a happy hunting ground existed here on earth. For the past two hundred years it was believed to exist at Fort Frances, Ontario, Kitchi'onahgumming.

Before the coming of the white man into this area there was an Ojibway Indian from Longlac, Ontario, who had a younger brother whom he loved very much. Their parents were both dead and there were only two of them. One day the younger brother died of some sickness and left the older very lonesome, but he knew his brother had gone to Kitchi'onahgumming, to the happy hunting ground there in Fort Frances. After he had put his brother's body in a safe place he left right away to try to bring back the soul of his departed brother, so that the body might live again.

It took time to get there, from Longlac to the mouth of the Pic River at Heron Bay, into Lake Superior and then to Fort Frances. When this Indian arrived he noticed a great village with canoes and well-travelled roads, but there was no one to be seen or heard. He waited until it was dark, and then he felt people present all around him and the shadows began to take shape. One of the souls of the departed made water on him, but he could not see anyone clearly.

Later, in one of the long houses, the Indian saw a bright light and heard drums pounding and a powwow. To get a better look he peeked inside

113

through a hole and then he noticed Indians who had been dead for a long time dancing and being very happy. He saw his parents, his grandfather and grandmother and other relatives, and his beloved brother who was dead.

When he had a chance he grabbed his brother's soul and placed it in a small box and headed for home. About half-way around Lake Superior the box, or the soul of his brother, spoke to him and said, "My brother, I know what great love you have for me and the sorrow you have for my loss. Consider, my brother, it would be of no use to take me back for I am now dead. Release me, my brother, to return where I shall be happy, and some day you will be with me for ever."

The brother, knowing and understanding that it was hopeless for anyone to live after their soul had left their body, opened the box. As soon it was open a noise was heard travelling very fast in the direction of Fort Frances, the place of the dead. A few years later this Ojibway Indian died of a broken heart, for his sorrow at his loss was too great, and he went to join his brother.

When the white man came into the area the place of the dead moved to another spot but now it is not known where it went, perhaps to the far beyond or to some other place unknown to anyone.

About a hundred years ago or more there lived at Kenogamashish Lake in the Longlac area an Ojibway couple, man and wife, who had a son, their only child, who was sick and had a malformed back. Apart from this he was very intelligent, clever and handsome. His name was Bright Sky and he was about twenty years old at the time this took place. One early spring he died.

The parents were lost under this great misfortune and their sorrow at the death of their only son. According to the custom of the time, they wrapped the body in big sheets of birchbark, for boards were unknown in those days. The burial ground was in one of the sandy beaches at this lake, near where today the cars go across the bridge on Highway Number 11 at Geraldton.

On this day the ice of the early spring gathered up at the burial ground and they were unable to bury their son and had to wait a couple more days until the warm winds melted or blew the ice to another direction. That same evening around four o'clock the father of the dead man left his wife alone in the wigwam, to hunt the geese that were plentiful at the opening of this lake.

Meanwhile the old lady was crying beside the body of her son until her husband returned and stood outside the wigwam. As she was wiping her tears a scratching noise was heard as if someone were scratching the bark. She did not pay any attention until it came a second time. Then, knowing what she heard but being afraid also, she called her husband to come inside and said, "Do you believe what I heard?"

When the two of them were sure, they opened up the wrappings and looked at their son who had been dead for three days. It was hard to believe. He was now looking at them but was unable to move except for his eyes and his fingers. It took quite a while to bring him to his normal feelings and enable him to speak, for his throat was dry. They gave him a great amount of fish soup and broth, until two days later Bright Sky was able to speak. The first thing the parents asked was, "Did you know that you were dead for three days?" And the son said he did not know for sure, but felt he was and now was sure. He had believed it was all a dream.

He was asked if he went any place, and now, knowing that he had been dead, he said, "Yes, I went to the place of the Great Manitou, for his voice was like many waters, so wonderful to hear, and it spoke to me in Indian. I could not see the Great Spirit for I saw only a great majestic brightness that was the Spirit itself, wisdom of all ages.

"The Great Wisdom said, 'Bright Sky, I command you to return, for it is not time for you to come here to heaven. Go home, for your back will not make you sick again, since you have died and your sickness cannot return with you. I am the Great Father of the Ojibway people. I love you, my children, but there are many things that I do not like that you all do, and I want you to go and pray. And when you have prayed then you shall come, never to return in your human body again.' "

Bright Sky did not know what prayer or praying was. Indians at that time did not know what Christianity was, for there was no one to teach them the salvation of God. The only thing the Ojibway people of this area knew was conjuring, their ancient Ojibway beliefs and playing drums to all the Ojibway medicine societies. Nevertheless, I will say here now that all the respected Ojibway tribes had some kind of worship and firmly believed in God, one God. But to pray as the Great Spirit said was new to this Indian. Also the Great Spirit said, "I do not like many things you do." I believe the Great Manitou accepted their form of worship to him, but still there were others who did conjuring that God did not like.

Bright Sky began to lead a good, respected life. He got married and tried to set a good example to all. The Indians of this area were very amazed by this great return from the dead and believed Bright Sky, but still there was no one to teach them the true salvation.

About three years later two Ojibway runners came to that area to bring good news to all, and said that the Indians at Pic River at Lake Superior were now joining a new religion. It was called praying to the Great Manitou and to Jesus Christ. It was preached and taught by the Black Robes carrying a cross, or crucifix. At the time the Great Spirit told Bright Sky to go and pray, the Spirit had said, "Look before you. You will see things that will be used for prayer." He saw crucifixes, a Bible, the purple cloth worn by the priest when hearing confession and the piece the priest puts on his arm during mass. All these things the runners mentioned to Bright Sky. The Ojibway Indians were glad to hear the great news. That summer the Indian people saw the men of God, whom they called the Black Robes in Ojibway. Indians all around accepted this new religion, for Bright Sky had taught them in advance to believe in it. At last salvation and a more pleasing way to pray to God were taught to all.

Bright Sky lived to be a hundred years old and had a lot of sons and daughters and grandchildren. He prayed all his life. Then he died but did not return again. I believe the Great Manitou was now very pleased with him.

The same thing happened to an Ojibway of the Lake Nipigon area who died long ago. This took place after the Black Robes had spread the good news of Christianity. This Indian was also believed to have died but was revived and afterwards was able to speak. He was asked if he went any place and said he did, as he well knew that he was dead. This is his version of what took place.

"In my journey to the great beyond I saw two roads, one very white road and the other a red road. I was asked to choose my road. For a while I did not know which to follow. Finally I decided to take the white road. I learned later that I made the right choice, for I am on the right road.

"I walked for a long time until I reached a very high wall, a great majestic fence. Upon getting there I saw the keeper of the gate, and he spoke to me and said, 'My son, I know that you are a believer in God and a good Christian. You are very young, however, only about eighteen years old. Go back to your earthly form and return here some other time,' and the keeper returned to his station."

The Ojibway said that he was exceedingly sorry to leave this place, for from the other side of the wall came the laughter of many happy people and music that was so good to hear and a brightness as if

117

the sun were shining ten times brighter. But here there was no sun.

He was advised to follow the red road back. On his way he noticed a man sitting on a chair who had horns on his head. Now he knew it was the Devil himself. But the Ojibway lad was not afraid and asked, "Which way shall I go to return to my earthly form?"

Satan replied, "Follow this road. You will see three things, two natural creatures and the third a pillar of fire. Touch this pillar of fire for it will be your body."

Before leaving he took a look and saw a great fire burning below in which perhaps is the so-called hell. Going on his way he came upon a big river crossed by a very narrow board. He noticed the ghostly bones of people who had tried to cross this river but were unable to make it, because they were either too old or too young to balance themselves on this narrow board. But for him it was easy to go across.

On the road he approached two huge dogs sitting side by side. The dogs wagged their tails at the lad for they knew that he always respected dogs and had never mistreated one in his entire life. If he had, perhaps it would have been really hard for him to pass, for the dogs were there to help those who treated their dogs well. This is one of the Ojibway beliefs, that everyone must try to take good care of dogs in the best possible way.

At last the road ended, and facing the Ojibway stood a pillar of fire. He tried to touch the fire but it burned his hands. He looked ahead and behind, but there was no road except where he was standing with the pillar of fire in front. Again he did what he was told to do, and this time his fingernail scorched on the pillar and all at once he knew that he was inside a coffin at home. Then he was revived and told this story of his true experience. He lived to a grand old age and had a wife and children and grandchildren. I believe that when he died at

last the keeper let him in to enjoy what he had
heard over the great wall.

In olden times the Ojibway Indians believed
there was a broad river leading to the great beyond,
or place of the dead. In this river was a stick floating back and forth. When an Indian died he would
jump from one side of the river to the other, and
it was believed that by means of this stick many
who failed to get across lived again and returned
to their earthly bodies after having been two days
gone. Young children, especially, came back alive,
due to the fact that they did not have enough power
to jump to the other side.

After the white man came, one Indian came back
alive again with good news and said, "No one has
to worry about the stick any more, for now a big
construction job is being done there. A great
majestic bridge is being built, so that it will be possible for even the very old to crawl across to the
happy hunting ground and for the very young to
run across the bridge." Now no one worries about
the stick. I take my hat off in respect and thanks to
the white man's Acme Construction Company for
building that bridge.

The great Ojibway people of North America believed there was one God, Gitchi Manitou, who was
their only God and whom they worshipped. The
Ojibway believed that there were six layers of
heaven. One to four were reserved for all the respected tribes of the Indian people, the fifth heaven
was reserved for people who had white skins and
the sixth layer was for the Great Spirit and his
company alone. The Ojibway had medicine
dreams about all these layers except the sixth layer.
No mind could penetrate to this place that was
reserved for the Great Spirit. In all the four layers
there were Ojibway or Indian guardians, who wore
scarlet clothing with pointed hoods like caps,
Heaven People to guard these heavens set aside
for all Indian people.

Each Indian went to one of these layers according to the way he behaved himself on earth. Everyone went to heaven no matter what he did; after all there was lots of room on the four layers. God is good and there was no such belief as hell. We do not believe there could be such a place. God, the giver of life, is all-good in every way and we cannot believe he would make the place called hell by our white brothers. Also although it is said from time to time in history that we were all a bunch of savages and needed the salvation of God very badly, I believe the Ojibway had the best belief about heaven. Where those of white origin went if they did wrong I cannot say. After all, this book concerns only Indian people, especially the Ojibway.

I myself, living in this modern era, believe no one knows where heaven is, but my people, the great Ojibway, often tried to find out. I have given you some idea of our beliefs. Even if these do not all sound convincing, at least I can say we had good imaginations.

People say that heaven is up in the great skies beyond the stars. If a rocket ship left the earth today, I understand it would travel for a long time and still not reach anywhere, for space is vast. As for those of my people who claimed to have gone some place after they were dead and then came back in a matter of two to three days, my idea is, where could they have gone? If the rocket ship could travel for ever without finding heaven, then there must be a heaven right here on earth that we pass every day without being able to penetrate its invisible wall. When a human body dies, however, and the soul leaves the body, then the soul itself can pass through this wall that we cannot pass in our human bodies.

Let me explain. We pass this wall every day. We never bump against it, but still it is there. Our human body could never go into what is on the other side of that wall, but a soul could penetrate it. If a soul that left this earth and pene-

Interdependence: Beaver and Human Life

trated the wall looked back, it would see a different place. But there would still be a wall in heaven, too, and it could be the earth on the other side.

So this I believe is the way a person goes after he is dead. If there is no wall, though, there must be a lot of souls travelling yet that have never reached their destination, unless the soul itself travels faster than a rocket ship.

According to an Ojibway story, there was a medicine-man called Blue Jay who claimed that he had visited the layers of heaven in a medicine dream. His guardian spirit, one of the Heaven People of the Ojibway belief, took him to the four layers reserved for Indians, where he saw Red Bird, Medicine Turtle, Bright Sky and many other chiefs and warriors whom he recognized, all arrayed in the best of feathers and clothing. He also told about the fifth layer of heaven set aside for the white-skinned people.

Blue Jay said, "In my dream I went into this layer of heaven, where I saw only white-coloured people who were dressed in the best of materials, in silk and satin in all colours of red, gold, yellow and blue. They did not have black hair as we have, but hair of lighter shades. I have never seen anyone look so white, except the traders. I did not see any of our people in this layer."

What is about to be told actually happened in Lake Nipigon sixty years ago. This Blue Jay was a great medicine-man with great medicine powers. In his days of fasting, when he was young, no one yet knew what dreams he had to make him believe he was a sort of god. Upon his becoming a medicine-man and a conjurer, the more knowledge he gained in medicine the more he believed he was high and mighty. As he grew older his conjuring became more serious. His guardian spirits in medicine told him that he was the greatest conjurer and medicine-man.

His style of conjuring was to fire a shot into the air and, just like the guided missile of today, the bullet was guided by his guardian spirits in medicine to wherever his enemy was, until it reached its destination and struck dead the person for whom it was intended.

When his time came, he died of old age but before he died he told his family and relatives, "Do not bury my body for I will return in three days." They waited three days for the return of Blue Jay, but he never returned. They took his body to an island on Lake Nipigon and they travelled from home to the island every day, but still Blue Jay never returned.

The Ojibway Indians believe in the reincarnation of a dead person, whereby his soul lives on in another life among his own people. I do not believe all Ojibway reincarnate, only those who have not passed a barrier. Important people such as medicine-men or chiefs have no special advantage, as anyone has the right. I have also heard that the soul could return by its own power if it wanted to.

As a Catholic, I am told we never reincarnate but prepare in this world for the next. It is a good, wholesome thought, but I respect the ancient Ojibway beliefs, and being an Indian and also having an intelligent mind, I do say now that I believe in the reincarnation of Ojibway Indians in accordance with the ancient teachings of my people. As for my Christian faith, that has no place in this book.

A modern Ojibway elder believes in souls that were in-between. A man who in life never accepted either the Christian faith or the ancestral faiths of his forefathers was an Indian of no faith. Upon his death he would ascend to heaven, his ancestral heaven of the Ojibway beliefs that had its opening here in Canada, a door that all Indians went through.

The Great Manitou of all Indian tribes would say to the soul, "As an Indian, by rights you should enter heaven's door here. But you did not practise the faith of your ancestors, you adopted the faith of the white man, Christianity. Go where they have their opening."

Then the soul goes to England, where the white man comes from. Upon arriving at that door where the white man enters, the God of the Christian faiths says, "Although you have practised the faith of my teachings faithfully, have observed my laws and lived a good life, being an Indian you cannot enter this door. For only the white race goes in here, not Indians. Go back to Canada and go to that door."

Then the soul wanders from place to place, trying the doors of all faiths, and it is not allowed to come in. For the Chinese, Buddhists or Moslems cannot let the Indian soul in. So what can it do?

I was told that the Indian then goes to the south to join his fellow Indians who have adopted Christian faiths and have forsaken their ancestral beliefs. The place the Indian goes is like a big burned-out forest where crowds of human souls wander.

Finally, with all other hope gone, the Indian's last chance is to reincarnate so that he may live again, this time in that belief in which he would be reborn. Then he is able to enter heaven.

The Ojibway belief states that Indians of the Ojibway reincarnate into another body and my people believe this without fear, except those who were brainwashed by the missionaries who claimed to have the one true religion.

My writing is not intended to mislead anybody. I write what I was told in good faith. I am not worried by what I have written for I know God is good. No matter if he is God or Manitou, he is the same Father of all humans and has one door for all colours to go into, without discrimination.

THE
SOCIETY OF HEAVEN
PEOPLE

In some parts of Ontario there are Ojibway Indians who claim to belong to the Society of Heaven People. Some call it the Wahbeenowin Society—the Vision Society. The Ojibway belief states that in heaven there are what the Indians of this society call Heaven People, Okeezhikokah Eninnewuk. These are guardians of heaven, not angels, but people who are Indians with fairer skin and, as I have said, dressed in scarlet tunics with a hood. The members of this society dress in the same manner as the Heaven People at their rites and ceremonies and great feasts, and hold dances in their honour. Each members believes he is going to heaven and has a number printed or punched with a nail on a half-moon badge made out of tin or other metal. This badge is worn on the hood, and it is believed that when a member dies the real Heaven People will ask the supernatural body what number it has, and upon submitting that number it will be admitted to heaven. Of course this society is centuries old.

Some Ojibway perform these rites and beliefs of olden time, others have different ones. I am talking about one particular tribe of Ojibway in this chapter and no names or places are mentioned for certain reasons of my own, as I am an Ojibway and some secrets cannot be told.

Some members never pray in any Christian church. To do this would make matters worse, as no member can go to heaven praying like a Christian and members of this society have to abide by the rules. Some will keep the rules, others will add something different, but each member is asked to try to lead a good life, follow the respected beliefs faithfully, and attend dances in honour of the Heaven People. In this way each one will get to heaven. In the graveyard where these members are buried no Christian influence, such as crosses or tombstones, is visible but at each grave there will be flags and ribbons, and this is the way members are buried and in that manner they will be saved.

No one is forced to join this society unless he wishes to do so. But if he is a Christian and was baptized, a new member upon joining would be asked to go into a steam house to purify his body and soul from the Christian baptismal influence, because if he is a Christian he would never go to heaven even if he were a full-fledged member. That is what I understand.

I spoke to a member some years back and we got into a good conversation concerning the Society of Heaven People in the area. He lived according to his basic belief. He told me it is now four generations since the society was founded. "The first man who founded this religion, or society, among my people four generations ago," stated the old man I spoke to, "had at that time six wives, as he was a good provider and a powerful medicine-man of great knowledge. Each wife had her own dwelling and had a lot of sons as well as daughters."

One day when the founder was about ninety years old, he called together at his bedside his followers of the Society of Heaven People, as well as his wives, sons and daughters, and said to them, "Tomorrow I will be dead, as I have been told in a dream by the Guardian of Heaven that it is time to get another to replace me, for I am too old to carry on my work. When I am dead do not ever give up your beliefs in the Wahbeenowin Society or its related societies. If any member falls out of his clan, or society, he shall be lost from the fold. I want each one of you to live according to our beliefs, to love one another, to try to live a good life, to have feasts and dances in honour of the Heaven People and to purify yourselves in body and soul each year. Lastly I want you to choose a member from generation to generation to hold firm to the belief we have now." (There were no Christian beliefs at that time.) "And now, my children, I am going to die and I will be going to heaven and someone will come to get my body and soul. So don't bury me when I am dead. Take me to the small island out in the lake and cover me with birchbark, and I want you all to sit by the shores to see who will come and get me."

Next morning the elder was dead and his last wish was carried out. They placed him on a small island about twelve o'clock that day. The great medicine pipe was lit for each one to smoke. When this was finished a great wind was heard from the very heavens. As it was clear and the skies were all blue and there were no clouds in sight everyone looked about, but the trees and the water remained calm. Again the wind was heard. Up in the sky a big opening was seen as if two walls began to open up. There appeared standing on a cloud four men dressed in scarlet clothing with pointed hoods on their heads. One was carrying a large flag of red and white. Another, carrying a big drum, started pounding it and sang a sacred song of the Heaven People. The remaining two came down as if walking down a ladder and stood about two feet above the ground and came toward the elder. One got hold of the birchbark sheet and one got hold of the dead elder. As everyone remained watching, seated by the shores, the elder was seen to come alive and looked at all his people for one more time.

Now the two scarlet-clothed men took hold of the elder and started to climb the invisible stairs. And when they all got to the top of the cloud the wall of the sky itself closed for ever. "Now," said the member who told me this happening, "we all hold this belief, for we know our founder was taken beyond the wall that is known as heaven. I am the fourth generation and when I am dead another will take my place."

I asked what he thought of the Christian belief and that Christ had said, "No one shall be saved by any other means except the Lord."

He replied in a respectful manner, "If people are to be saved by Christ then they will be saved, but if we believe in our belief that I have told you of we shall be saved by that faith also." I thanked him and let the subject drop.

There lived at one time around Red River, Manitoba, a medicine-man of the Ojibway tribe who was known for his great magic in bringing back those who were dead.

One Indian of Lake Nipigon married a woman from the Red River area, and after many years of married life together a misfortune occurred in the family. One of their older daughters died of TB. The Indian, being a good Christian at the time, did not believe in the magic of the so-called medicine of the Ojibway conjuring. His wife spoke to him and said, "My husband, let us go to my homeland and seek the medicine-man of my tribe. For he is great and he could bring back our daughter for us to see once again before she goes for ever to the great beyond." So the kindly Indian said to his wife, "We will go," just to please her, as she was broken-hearted.

Their journey took time and when they arrived they were welcomed by the woman's relatives, and the medicine-man got everything arranged for the next day. Before playing the great medicine drum that he would use to summon the dead girl, the medicine-man said, "Everyone is to be seated in a great circle and those who wish to see the visitors from heaven, including the dead woman, must pay ten dollars for one eye and twenty dollars for two eyes. Those who pay ten dollars will see with only one eye, and those who don't pay anything will bow their heads to the ground and close their eyes. If anyone peeks it will affect the vision."

Everything was in order and a great medicine pipe was passed around for those that smoked this pipe with clear and honest hearts. Then four drummers in scarlet clothing, representing the Heaven People Society, were seated and the medicine-man started to sing. The skies were clear with not a cloud in sight, and the winds were very calm. All was still. Then about five hundred feet ahead of them the sand on the ground began to twist as if a light wind were blowing from the heavens. Suddenly in front of them appeared a light that moved back and forth until it became very clear. There, about two feet above the ground, stood two men dressed in the scarlet clothing of the Heaven People.

Between them was the daughter whom her parents had come to see. Now she appeared to be very happy and good-looking, and pointed toward the blue sky. She did not speak. The mother's heart was joyful and she was contented to see her daughter looking so happy. In about three or four minutes the medicine vision disappeared, not to be seen again. And this is a great mystery among my people, the Ojibway.